Praise for *The Trustworthy Leader*

"Amy Lyman shows that trust is not something that rare folks just *happen* to create. Instead, her stories of incredible corporate leaders show how their core commitments run deep and their practices build powerful trust, which in turn generates consistently exceptional results. Lyman offers nothing short of a path to greatness."

—Daniel Mulhern, Distinguished Practitioner of Business, Haas School of Business, University of California, Berkeley

"Amy Lyman has a wealth of experience and data to show us how to create and maintain trustworthy employee relations, which benefits both employees and the firm's bottom line. An enlightening read!"

—Doug Kruse, professor, Rutgers University School of Management and Labor Relations

"Amy Lyman gets it! She understands that trust is the heart of creating a successful organization and strong relationships. Need help being the best leader you can be? Start working on the foundation—trust."

—Elizabeth R. James, vice chairman, CPO, and CIO (retired), Synovus Financial Corp.

"Want to know the lessons of leaders whose companies make the FORTUNE 100 Best Companies to Work For list? Let Amy Lyman include you in her highly readable conversation about their ideas, their companies, their aspirations, and their challenges. These leaders are serious about leading great organizations, and this book brilliantly tells their stories. What a wonderfully learned book!"

—Joseph R. Blasi, J. Robert Beyster Professor, Rutgers University School of Management and Labor Relations

THE TRUST WORTHY LEADER

Leveraging the Power of Trust to Transform Your Organization

Amy Lyman

JOSSEY-BASS
A Wiley Imprint
www.josseybass.com

Published by Jossey-Bass
A Wiley Imprint
One Montgomery Street, Suite 1200, San Francisco, CA 94104-4594
www.josseybass.com

Jossey-Bass books and products are available through most bookstores. To contact Jossey-Bass directly call our Customer Care Department within the U.S. at 800-956-7739, outside the U.S. at 317-572-3986, or fax 317-572-4002.

Wiley also publishes its books in a variety of electronic formats and by print-on-demand. Some material included with standard print versions of this book may not be included in e-books or in print-on-demand. If the version of this book that you purchased references media such as CD or DVD that was not included in your purchase, you may download this material at http://booksupport.wiley.com. For more information about Wiley products, visit www.wiley.com.

Library of Congress Cataloging-in-Publication Data
Lyman, Amy.
    The trustworthy leader : leveraging the power of trust to transform your organization / Amy Lyman.—1st ed.
        p. cm.
    Includes bibliographical references and index.
    ISBN 978-0-470-59628-9 (cloth); ISBN 978-1-118-15765-7 (ebk); ISBN 978-1-118-15766-4 (ebk); ISBN 978-1-118-15767-1 (ebk)
    1. Leadership. 2. Management. 3. Trust. 4. Organizational behavior. I. Title.
    HD57.7.L94 2012
    658.4'092—dc23

                                                            2011035622

Printed in the United States of America
FIRST EDITION
HB Printing   10 9 8 7 6 5 4 3 2 1

This book is dedicated to Marc Simon and Simeon Lyman-Levering.

Thank you for all you have given me, for how you have helped me to learn and grow, and always for the trust we share.

CONTENTS

PREFACE

I have long been fascinated with leadership and the qualities that distinguish excellent leaders from those who try, yet don't quite reach those heights. I have worked for a few great leaders—people who inspired and challenged everyone to do more, to try harder, to use our brains and talents. I've also worked for leaders who did not measure up.

Although I'd had both successful and not-so-successful examples of leadership on which to reflect, when it was my turn to be in a leadership position, I experienced the role of leader from yet a new perspective. Like many people, I brought personal strengths with me yet I did not see myself as a natural leader. Nor did I have the inclination or perseverance to develop into a great one. My attention was always more drawn to researching the practices of other leaders, observing and assessing people's responses, analyzing employee survey and focus group data, and sharing my findings. My time in leadership positions became invaluable to my research efforts, as my personal experience affirmed for me many of the challenges leaders face. It also gave me new insights into the skills, talents, and commitments of great leaders.

Over the years, I have worked with many people who have wanted to become successful, Trustworthy Leaders. I have learned that those people who succeed do so because their talents, ability, willingness to learn, and desire to lead propels them to success. I've also learned that the most successful leaders exemplify a consistent integrity between their actions and their words. A leader who simply mouths the words yet shows no ability to put them into practice creates a demoralized or disenchanted workforce. Trustworthy Leaders commit themselves to live up to the highest aspirations found in their words.

Although there is more to leadership than this, the central concept of integrity between actions and words drives the success of the Trustworthy Leaders I've studied. But how and around what content? What is it that is so singular about these leaders that causes people to choose to follow them? I committed to uncovering the qualities and characteristics of great leaders. I wanted to understand and document their experiences and discover exactly what makes them so special. I did this to satisfy my own curiosity and so that you could learn from these great leaders as well. And that's how this book was born.

I first began my extensive research on why great leaders are able to create positive outcomes for themselves and their organizations— and on what exactly they do well—by digging deep into the leadership literature. What I found is a mixed bag. Many books and studies focus on how leadership actions lead to the end result of high profits or high status, without uncovering the foundation of leadership that contributes to an organization's ability to be positive, profitable, and successful. Although a reasonable level of profits is absolutely essential to the successful functioning of any organization, leaders do not "lead" money; they lead people. And it is through great people leadership that organizations succeed and become great themselves.

In a good portion of the leadership literature, great people leadership is not acknowledged as the key to success. Yet there is some research that speaks poignantly to this heart of leadership. These studies and reports identify the unique qualities and characteristics of people who are seen as great leaders, tying those qualities back to the outcomes essential to organizational success. It is this material that provided support for my deepening understanding of the role of trust in leadership success.

The most significant influence on my understanding of leadership, however, did not come from reading books and articles, nor did it come through my own professional experiences with leadership. Rather, my strong views on leadership have come from the more than twenty years I've spent working with people in great companies through my work at the Great Place to Work Institute, which I cofounded in 1991 and which today continues to help companies transform their workplace culture.

The Institute is best known for its role in researching and selecting the 100 Best Companies that appear each year in *Fortune* magazine. A group of international affiliates also produces similar lists for their markets. The Institute's first work, before the lists came out in *Fortune*, began with consulting and educational services. People wanted to know how to create great workplaces, and they came to the Institute to find out. And this is where I spent much of my time.

Our Trust Index—the survey that we designed during the early days of the Institute to measure the quality of relationships between employees and their leaders and managers—has provided me with an abundance of data. In 2011 in the United States alone, we received 40,000 responses to the Trust Index from employees in companies that made it onto the *Fortune* 100 Best Companies to Work For list. Close to 100,000 responses came in from employees in companies that applied to the list but didn't make it. And over 40,000 more came from employees in companies that made it onto the Institute's Best Small & Medium Companies to Work For list. I have suffered from no data shortage over the years of my consulting and research work, and I was able to call on this rich information while writing this book.

In addition to analyzing these Trust Index survey results, I also reviewed hundreds of "Culture Audits" for my research. When companies apply for the 100 Best Companies list, they answer a series of closed and open-ended questions about the organization's demographics, structure, benefits, and guiding philosophy and values. This information makes up the Culture Audit. I have been studying both the Trust Index and Culture Audit data for years, looking at survey response patterns, reading employee comments, examining shifts and long-standing trends, looking for the story all of this information has to tell.

Specifically for this book, I conducted a series of interviews with leaders at many of the companies that have earned a spot on one of the Institute's Best Companies lists. Although I am a strong believer in the power of combining quantitative and qualitative data to tell a story, in this book I've avoided almost completely the numbers, charts, and graphs I often use in my articles and presentations. Though quantitative data is incredibly valuable, and you need to know the numbers to support planning, forecasting, and tracking, numbers alone will not move your organization forward. Currently leaders are inundated with too many numbers and receive too little support for their own personal development of the leadership qualities that will actually help them to lead. What we need now are more overarching theories—based in solid research and backed up with real stories to offer guidance—and more analysis of the actions that work. That's what I provide in *The Trustworthy Leader.*

The interviews I conducted with leaders across industries allowed me to explore in detail a number of recurring themes about leadership. They provided me with the heart of what I share with you in the rest of this book. The topics I discussed with the interviewees included the challenges faced by leaders and how each leader's perspective guided their decision making at critical times. The leaders' stories echoed the themes that I heard twenty years ago when I first started talking with people about their experiences in great workplaces. Back then, as now, leaders talked about the importance of trust, of acknowledging people, of being supported and supporting others, of seeing people as human beings first and employees second—of being *trustworthy*.

Putting these interviews together with decades of experience and observation, I am able to state clearly what it is about Trustworthy Leaders that sets them apart and makes them so successful. In *The*

Trustworthy Leader, I share this knowledge with you, so that more and more of you will become Trustworthy Leaders and make a difference in workplaces all around the world.

San Francisco, California   Amy Lyman
October 2011

CHAPTER ONE

THE TRUSTWORTHY LEADER

Some of the more poignant moments in my consulting career have come during discussions with leaders and their "people" person (often a representative from Human Resources) as they seek help motivating employees to take on the next challenge. The difficult part of these discussions comes when leaders ask me how to fit time for people issues into their busy schedules. They then await the golden answer they hope I can provide that will help them to convince staff that they care.

One particularly memorable discussion took place after I had surveyed the employees at a large insurance company about their workplace experience. The CEO, vice president of Human Resources, and I were meeting briefly prior to my presentation of the survey results to the entire senior management team. The VP of HR, sitting to my right, leaned into the conversation and asked me what the CEO, on my left—a very busy man—could do if he had only five minutes each day to devote to people issues.

I was a bit stunned by the question. Five minutes is barely enough time to greet a single employee and ask him how he's doing, let alone show support for people's growth and development, convey your vision as a leader, and provide people with a sense of direction. And this company had over ten thousand employees!

I turned to the CEO on my left and addressed him directly. "Leading is a full-time job," I said. "If you want to be successful as a leader, you need to devote *all* of your time to people issues. Strategy, product development, customer service, innovation—they all depend on people. Five minutes a day—or even five minutes an hour—is the wrong approach."

Initially taken aback by my directness, the CEO was now paying attention. He also heard in my response the resolution to a dilemma he experienced. He said he was not comfortable switching on his usual care and concern for people at certain times and then switching it off when he considered strategic decisions, business partnerships, financial opportunities, or marketing proposals. Yet all of his management training, and many of his peers, had encouraged him to do just that—respond to people issues when asked, yet focus his intellectual talents on the mechanics of the specific tasks in front of him.

I reminded him that people were integral to his ability to be successful in every single arena within his organization and that if he did not include consideration of people in every aspect of his work, then he was doing himself and the organization a great disservice.

He paused for a moment, mulling this over before responding. What I had said made sense, yet no one had ever said it so directly. He understood himself and his role as a leader well enough to know that clarity and consistency in actions and words is important for successful leadership. He had also previewed the employee survey report and knew that people had raised concerns about actions they felt were inconsistent with his stated goal of creating a great workplace. The question now was what to do about it.

The answer was both simple and complex: this leader needed to focus on being trustworthy.

WHAT IT MEANS TO BE TRUSTWORTHY

For the past twenty years I have listened to people talk about the importance of trust in their workplace relationships and of the devastating effects of its absence on productivity, job satisfaction, and commitment.

In 1991, I cofounded the Great Place to Work Institute, best known for its role in researching and selecting the "100 Best Companies to Work For" feature that appears each year in *Fortune* magazine. Prior to the lists in *Fortune*, the Institute was known for its work promoting the concept that great workplaces could be created by focusing on the development of trust between leaders/managers and employees. A book about the 100 Best Companies was published in 1984,[1] and initial financial analysis comparing the performance of the Best Companies to their industry peers showed strong evidence that the 100 Best were better financial performers as well as better workplaces. A related book, *A Great Place to Work*, published in 1988,[2] laid out the analytical framework for creating great workplaces. It is from this book that the initial ideas for the Institute were developed.

People began paying attention to the possibility of creating great workplaces, and the Institute's work had a ready audience. I spent much of my time developing the consulting and advising services that helped leaders understand why trust is so important to organization success, and also how they themselves could become more trustworthy. Leaders saw that they could become stronger leaders by being trustworthy and could also increase the likelihood of success for their organizations.

During the early years at the Institute, my colleagues and I developed and used an employee survey as our primary data source—a tool designed to ascertain the quality of relationships between employees and their leaders and managers. That survey, now called the Trust Index, is used around the world by the Great Place to Work Institute and international affiliates that produce Best Company lists for their markets. To develop and refine the survey, we used the first-person employee interviews conducted for the original *100 Best Companies to Work For* book and the research for *A Great Place to Work*.

We had the luxury of time to develop the Trust Index, so we were able to study the interview transcripts in great detail. We noted that three elements came up again and again in the words of employees when they described why they trusted their managers and leaders: credibility, respect, and fairness. Therefore, our first goal in developing the survey tool was to accurately capture employees' perceptions of the credibility of their leaders, the respect with which they felt treated, and their experience of the fairness of workplace policies and practices. To this day, when asked why their workplace is great, employees who have never seen a description of the Great Place to Work model or heard the Institute's definition of a great workplace—one where "you trust the people you work for, have pride in what you do, and enjoy the people you work with"—speak of *the power of trust*. And when employees are asked to tell stories about how they experience trust, as they reflect on the behavior of their leaders, the words *credible*, *respectful*, and *fair* come up all the time.

WHAT IS TRUST?

We use the word *trust* to explain a bond that is created between and among people. Trust is an emotional and a cerebral connection, characterized by an ability to rely on someone to act in ways that will be of benefit to one's own health and well-being. Trust often comes into play during challenging times, when stress, miscommunication, or poorly conceived actions place a strain on people's bonds. Trust is what helps people to have faith that they can work through the challenges and arrive at a positive outcome. Trust-based relationships are also deeply enjoyable, as they bring comfort and stability, with the experience of trust providing support to the relationship and contributing to an individual's sense of security and belonging.

Trust develops through interaction. An interaction can be a conversation between two people, a look that passes between a father and child, or collective hard work among a group of people rebuilding a home. These actions convey a willingness on the part of one person to do something that is of benefit to another's health and well-being. The more the actions are repeated, the deeper the connection developed, and the greater the likelihood of a long-term trust relationship.

In the workplace, trust can infuse every element of a leader's actions. Even if a leader isn't obviously engaging in a trust-building action—if, say, she's just going down the hallway to refill her coffee cup—her interactions with those she passes en route reflect on her trustworthiness. Does she make eye contact? Say anything? How do the people she acknowledges respond? With a sharp focus on the details, even a minor coffee break can be seen as fertile ground for trust-building.

And a sharp focus is exactly what has been used at the Great Place to Work Institute to study people's experience of trust in the workplace. Actions that build trust affirm a person's credibility, convey respect to others, and embody a spirit of fairness in their implementation. Everyone is capable of acting in ways that will lead to the creation of trust. Everyone. When we act in ways that convey our credibility, show respect to others, and affirm a commitment to fairness, we are showing others that we are trustworthy.

As commonsensical as all of this seems, there are still many leaders who struggle to develop trust-based relationships with their employees. Why?

THE MYTH OF THE SUCCESSFUL LEADER

For many years a stereotyped notion has reigned of the successful leader. This leader is portrayed as all-knowing, a bit greedy, a tough decision maker, and consumed with work. These are not generally the characteristics you'd want in a friend, yet these qualities have often been cited—and exaggerated—as prerequisites for business success. In this definition of the successful leader, "success" is equated with making considerable sums of money—for oneself and, ideally, for the company— and often living with the trappings of conspicuous consumption and excessive display. People who follow this leadership model are actually less successful in the eyes of their employees, who see the great distance between themselves and the person leading the enterprise and often feel that the leader's excesses come at their expense. This mythical leader is also less likely to create an organization that will be successful in the marketplace.

If the only goal of a business leader is to create a financially successful company, then he or she will want to be a Trustworthy Leader. Although Trustworthy Leaders do not choose to be trustworthy for the sole purpose of making more money, it is one of the notable benefits of building trust. My research and that of others confirms this. From 1998 through 2011, the publicly traded 100 Best Companies, as a group and over time, have outperformed the Russell 3000 and S&P 500, posting annualized returns of 11.06 percent versus 4.26 percent and 3.83 percent, respectively.[3] The primary factor that gets a company to be selected for the 100 Best Companies list is the level of trust between employees and management. As you'll see again and again throughout this book, Trustworthy Leaders lead fiscally sound companies, weather economic storms while their contemporaries struggle, attract and keep the best talent, and encourage high levels of innovation and problem solving.

Trustworthy Leaders are so successful because they *do* see beyond the goal of dollar signs. They understand the complexity of bringing together a group of human beings to pursue extraordinary accomplishments. They are masters at guiding, directing, encouraging, and challenging people to contribute their best, in part because they ask the same of themselves. Trustworthy Leaders know that their relationships with others throughout the organization are key to their success—however success is measured.

Trustworthy Leaders are also independent-minded enough to think for themselves and not just follow the pack. They choose to create their own leadership style and approach—one that is inclusive and respectful rather than one that is selfish and mercenary. At their core, Trustworthy Leaders believe in the inherent value and dignity of people—*all* people—a belief that influences their choices and guides their actions.

Most importantly, they understand that great leadership is a way of being, not something that can be switched on and off.

This new model that I was developing of the Trustworthy Leader— from the five-minute people person, through my deep understanding of the power of trust, to a challenge to the popular myth of leadership success—called for a compelling framework. As I considered what I was learning, I kept going back to the transcripts of my conversations with Trustworthy Leaders. I looked for the pattern in their experiences, the key moments when they understood the power of trust. I pushed myself to understand what had happened to them that set them on the path to being trustworthy. The pattern that emerged, illustrating the shared path of leaders who are widely considered trustworthy, is one in which aspirations are high, consequences are acknowledged, responsibility is accepted, and leaders move forward. I call this path the Virtuous Circle of Trustworthy Leadership.

THE VIRTUOUS CIRCLE

Usually we think of a path as a straight line from one point to another. Yet for most of us, our growth and development never moves forward in a straight line. There are always shifts and changes, times when things seem to speed up and other times when we feel stuck. There are lessons we circle back to even as we move forward. The Trustworthy Leader's path is similar, always moving forward, yet—as in our own lives—each step that leads to the next is connected to the previous one as well, creating a circular path of growth and learning. And as we complete one circle with some new experience, something to put into practice, we begin again, only stronger. The next round through the Virtuous Circle both reinforces and strengthens the lessons learned from the previous round.

There are six distinct elements in a Trustworthy Leader's Virtuous Circle that combine to both create and reflect his or her trustworthiness:

- Honor
- Inclusion
- Value and engage followers
- Sharing information
- Developing others
- Movement through uncertainty to pursue opportunities

Each of these elements both influences how a leader acts and reflects how that person thinks about being a leader. Thinking about what you are doing and the impacts that your actions have on others is a singular requirement of effective, Trustworthy Leadership.

The *honor* felt by Trustworthy Leaders is continuous and greatly influences their actions. Many of us feel honored when we receive an award or recognition for a special accomplishment or a contribution we've made to the good of others. Trustworthy Leaders extend this sense of being honored to their roles as leaders, expressing gratitude for being asked to lead and acknowledging the responsibility that comes with it.

The *inclusion* of all people in an organization's community is a hallmark of Trustworthy Leadership. A leader's active involvement in promoting the inclusion of every person into the larger community of the organization is critical. One of the most important ways that leaders accomplish this is by building bridges of trust that extend beyond the boundaries of individual departments or divisions. This is of great benefit to the enterprise that wants people across the entire organization to work well together.

The ability to *value* and actively *engage followers* is a further sign of leadership excellence. Great, Trustworthy Leaders engage those who are following them by paying attention to them and learning from them. They acknowledge people's choice to follow, seek to support their contributions, and connect with them as people beyond their work roles. They celebrate the leadership of followers who may take on specific projects or create new efforts that open markets or improve existing products and services. Evidence that a leader is trustworthy will come from his or her followers.

Trustworthy Leaders *openly share information* with people to help them participate in and influence the life of the organization. They invite people into discussions that will support the expansion of the organization's products and services. These leaders know that employees' contributions will be magnified to the degree that they have access to useful information.

A leader who is focused on *developing others* will help employees to learn, grow, and discover their talents. In great organizations with strong trusted leaders, career and professional development programs reach broadly and deeply throughout the organization, providing everyone with a path to travel. Developing people is part of the perspective of Trustworthy Leaders because they think about others more than they think about themselves.

Finally, the success of any organization is dependent on the leader's ability to *move through uncertainty and find opportunities.* The skillful weighing of risks and rewards attached to the opportunities available is one of the most important actions that leaders can take on. When employees see their leader act with honor, feel included, choose to follow, have access to information they can use, and are supported in their development, they will support the leader's efforts to try novel approaches and find the best way forward. They will do this from a place that is deeply embedded in their own values and the values of the organization. This provides Trustworthy Leaders with an incomparable advantage in the marketplace.

Given that these elements of the Virtuous Circle are key to understanding the Trustworthy Leader, we explore all of them in more detail in the following chapters.

WHAT THE TRUSTWORTHY LEADER LOOKS LIKE

You might be surprised to learn who Trustworthy Leaders are, and what they look like—and not because of any unexpected resumé trait, but because their resumés are all so different. They come from varied backgrounds and work in completely disparate industries. Many have the business pedigree you'd expect from a CEO, while others have worked their way up from positions such as security guard, part-time support staff, cashier, or stocking clerk. Still others have left jobs from far afield in order to take leadership positions in great organizations.

For example, Sally Jewell, the president and CEO of Recreational Equipment, Inc. (REI)—which has made the Great Place to Work Institute's list of 100 Best Companies each year since the list's inception—is known for her accomplishments, which fit the typical profile of a corporate leader. Yet Jewell completely shatters the profile when you consider her approach to leadership. Jewell is smart, assertive, and a bold decision maker. She is capable of holding detailed discussions not only about finance, retail marketing, and merchandising—which you would expect—but also about oil and gas engineering and banking, two industries with which she was previously associated. What sets Jewell apart, though, is her compassion, ability to listen, her attention to the lives of all employees, her deep understanding of the workings of human beings alone and in groups—and, most importantly, her use of all of this knowledge in her role as CEO. To put it simply, she brings her humanity to the workplace every day.

"There are some nonnegotiables that I've always followed," she says of being a Trustworthy Leader, a designation given to her by her colleagues. "Greet people authentically and say hello. Create a sense of safety for yourself and your team members so that all can work for the common good and shared success. Listen as an ally. Listen, listen, listen, and engage." She goes on to say, "I am naturally comfortable saying hello to everybody I meet. I make a point of not missing eye contact, and in some way, as long as it doesn't feel forced, to acknowledge that somebody's there. Whether or not I know their name, I am not going to walk by as if they don't exist."

In Jewell's case, greeting those she passes by comes naturally. But it doesn't come naturally to everyone. In fact, many qualities of

Trustworthy Leadership may not come naturally to you, but that doesn't mean they're out of your reach. "Several of my colleagues just do not see other people," says Jewell. "They are very focused and targeted on the people they are talking with [and thus can walk by other people without acknowledging them]. This can come across as aloof and dismissive. When that happens, I let them know, 'It is not optional for you to not say hello to the people you walk by. I know it does not come naturally, but you really need to practice.'"

Being visible and accessible and acknowledging employees is vital to Jewell's view of effective leadership. She puts as much emphasis on the development of a leader's openness and ability to connect with others as she does on the more traditional leadership skills of public speaking, operations management, or creating new product strategies. If one of the skills Jewell believes to be nonnegotiable isn't present, she'll work with the individuals to help them develop it. *Honor*, *inclusion*, and *developing others* are all embedded in this small slice of Jewell's vision.

Like Jewell, Dan Warmenhoven has a career profile that looks, on the surface, much like that of a prototypical CEO. He is ambitious and driven and has served in many significant leadership roles. Warmenhoven is now chairman of the board of directors at NetApp (the #1 Best Company to Work For in 2009, and #5 in 2011). He was NetApp's CEO from 2005 to 2009, and before that spent ten years as the company's president. During his tenure, he steered NetApp along an aggressive course to become one of the leading storage and data management companies in the world. Aside from his traditional business experiences and successes, Warmenhoven describes his Jesuit education—in which, along with standard coursework, he was taught the value of service to others—as having had a considerable impact on his leadership style.

When Warmenhoven first joined NetApp, it was a smaller company with the promise of a great idea—an idea in need of leadership. He took the company public in 1995, and over the next fifteen years he helped to create a culture of openness that fueled innovation and creativity as well as intense employee loyalty to the organization's mission. At the time of this book's publication, NetApp is closing in on $4 billion of worldwide revenue; it has roughly 5,500 employees in the United States and more around the world. And many, many people want to work there.

At an all-company meeting I attended in 2007, Warmenhoven spoke about the challenges the company was facing. He began by speaking broadly about what he was going to share—information about the company's financial performance, strategic initiatives, and competitive position—and then proceeded to emphasize the importance of trust. He reminded people that sharing information was key to ensuring that all the people in the company were well-informed and able to contribute their best to their shared success. He talked about the valuable and confidential nature of the information he was about to share, and the importance of everyone trusting each other and knowing that people would keep this information in-house. He specifically noted that the sharing of this type of information was a sign of the confidence that NetApp's leaders had in all the employees, of their importance to the enterprise, and of the faith that leaders had in employees' ability to use the information wisely. And then he shared, calling out people and departments and their roles. *Honor, inclusion, sharing information,* and *balancing uncertainty and opportunity* are the Virtuous Circle qualities most evident in this anecdote about Warmenhoven.

Jewell and Warmenhoven embody what a Trustworthy Leader can do. I also want to share a story that demonstrates how a leader's mastery of the Virtuous Circle can permeate an entire organization, making the whole enterprise stronger.

Griffin Hospital, a community-based hospital in Derby, Connecticut, has been recognized for years as a great workplace with a high-trust culture. As part of their efforts to always improve, the hospital conducts regular patient satisfaction surveys. In 2008, a survey revealed that a number of patients felt discomfort when they had blood drawn. So Griffin put plans in place to hire an external trainer to retrain all bedside staff in phlebotomy procedures. Griffin leaders shared this training plan with staff at a regular weekly staff meeting. When Tracy

Huneke, an emergency room technician, heard the news, she raised her hand and said that she was qualified to teach phlebotomy.

The very next day, Huneke met with Barb Stumpo, vice president of Patient Care Services, to talk about how she could lead the phlebotomy training efforts at Griffin. As Stumpo describes it, Tracy Huneke was a hidden gem; she was doing an excellent job in the emergency room, yet she clearly had much more to offer at Griffin. After Huneke's initial meeting with Stumpo, she began to develop curricular materials for training—and retraining—all bedside staff on phlebotomy procedures. Within one year, everyone had been retrained, and phlebotomy-related complaints were down to zero. Yet Huneke didn't stop there.

"She had a vision," Stumpo said. "She wanted to open a school where we could offer courses on phlebotomy and also branch out into other allied health professions. We put together a business plan and contacted the State of Connecticut. We were authorized at the end of August 2009 through the State of Connecticut Department of Higher Education, and shortly thereafter we began a twelve-week phlebotomy course open to the community. We have thirty-one students who are enrolled in both the day and evening program."

Huneke describes it: "I took it upon myself to launch this initiative and went forward with it. I worked on the plans for about a year and a half, completed the state application, and worked to get everything signed and approved. I couldn't be happier [with the results]. We're having fun, learning, and things are all coming together. We've received four grants for some simulation equipment [to expand the school's offerings], and I don't plan on stopping. It's been great."

This story demonstrates the real business benefits of the Virtuous Circle. Huneke spoke up, her clinical director listened, the director had easy access to senior leaders at Griffin (who practice open-door management), and the very next day the process started moving at warp speed. Huneke had a vision of ways in which she could contribute to the betterment of Griffin and to patients, her community, and her own future. Griffin's culture of openness and support—made possible by

Trustworthy Leadership—created an environment in which she was comfortable offering both her current skills and her aspirations.

Leaders at Griffin have always encouraged professional development, and the practice of *developing others* is a strong part of their Virtuous Circle. Without Trustworthy Leadership, the *sharing of information* that led to Huneke's learning about the phlebotomy training would not have happened. Griffin's strong commitment to the practice of *inclusion* helped Huneke feel comfortable about speaking up and volunteering to run the training, and a successful new business venture—being managed by an up-and-coming Trustworthy Leader—is now a reality.

WHAT NEXT: HOW TO USE THIS BOOK

If any of the examples of trustworthy behavior that I share with you in the pages that follow seem out of reach, rest assured that they are not. Trust is built over time, not overnight, and it takes a deep understanding of yourself and your values to develop successful trust-based relationships. As you come to understand the roots of trust, you will find that you have a rich source of lessons and experiences to learn from in your own life.

In addition to identifying the actions and values that contribute to the development of trust at a fundamental level, I want the stories in this book to inspire you. Great leaders come in many packages. The profiles of leaders you will see in this book are designed to show you how ordinary people have built extraordinary trust-based relationships throughout their work lives—and, as a result, extraordinary companies. To this end, I share stories about how these leaders came to understand the power of being trustworthy—what experiences and insights guided them, how they deepened their understanding of human nature, and how they have been able to take action in different ways, large and small, to create trust-based relationships. And I document how these leaders believe that being trustworthy contributes directly to the success of their organizations.

Through the stories of these Trustworthy Leaders, I want to show you a path. This path involves taking your own unique experiences, plus your positive beliefs about the inherent value of people, and combining them into a commitment to take action. Once you do, you will create strong, positive relationships throughout your organization that will support success and achievements at a level not possible without the presence of trust.

CHAPTER TWO

THE HONOR OF LEADERSHIP

In late 2001 the United States was gripped in the mystery and fear surrounding an inhalation anthrax scare that had swept across the country. It was a time when tensions were already high and nerves frayed by a number of significant events that had occurred previously. Griffin Hospital in Derby, Connecticut, cared for a patient who later died because of exposure to anthrax. Following this person's death, Griffin's CEO, Patrick Charmel, informed employees of what was happening, defying a strongly worded FBI request that he not inform employees until after the FBI had spent more time investigating. For Charmel, putting his employees first was a weighty choice, though ultimately an easy one. He had established trust with his employees, he respected them and their lives, and he had faith that if asked, they would not reveal the situation to outsiders until the all-clear signal had been given.

Charmel chose to honor Griffin's employees by letting them know what had happened to the patient, and by letting them know all the steps that the hospital was taking to ensure the safety of every employee. He acted honorably, with integrity toward the organization's values, and showed strong leadership by putting the needs and concerns of employees above those of high-ranking government officials. He is the leader of a group of people who trust him; he is honored to hold that role and honored by their trust in him.

This story engenders strong reactions from people who hear it. Many have wished that their own leaders would stand up for them in such a way and react positively. Yet the same story evokes nervous reactions from others who wonder how they would have acted if faced with a similar situation. Examples of these kinds of principled choices are presented throughout this chapter—indeed, throughout this book.

While leadership honor can show up in dramatic situations such as what happened at Griffin, it can also be seen in people's daily actions that convey the honor they find in fulfilling their immediate responsibilities. Trustworthy Leaders are proud of their accomplishments, just like most of us. Yet they spend more time talking about others' contributions to the success of their organizations than about anything that they may have done personally. They boast about the recent "extra effort" of some person in a department or division far from their own office, and they tell these stories with great enthusiasm. And because of someone else's extra effort, they also give more themselves. This aspect of great leaders—their ability to talk glowingly and sincerely of the accomplishments of others—exemplifies a quality of Trustworthy Leadership I have seen for many years: Trustworthy Leaders don't feel entitled to be where they are; they feel honored.

Honor is the perfect starting place for uncovering what makes a Trustworthy Leader distinct. A leader's sense of honor provides evidence of the quality of *relationships* that he or she has with people. In other words, the feeling of being honored is a reflection of the perceptions of others; it is not something that you create on your own, the way you can create self-discipline or fastidiousness, for example. It's not about how good a leader is or thinks she is; it's about how good *others* think she is.

Being a leader in an organization involves a specific set of acquired skills and resources—including knowledge, competence, and a willingness to act—that are often most visible when a decision needs to be made. The successful implementation of a decision relies on a different set of skills—often tactical and strategic. Both of these skill sets are frequently commented on by leadership scholars and cited as the key to leadership success. Yet during my interviews with Trustworthy Leaders, the distinguishing feature of their leadership was less about any particular skill set, and more about the sense of honor they brought to the position. For while many people can acquire useful leadership skills, far fewer seem to act from a foundation of honor when they use those skills.

During my interviews, I asked leaders to describe to me what they thought had happened to them, what experiences made them a person of whom others would say, "He's great," or "She's trustworthy," or "I feel respected by her." Their stories led me to understand the first element in the Virtuous Circle—honor—and the qualities of humility, reciprocity, and position awareness that make up a leader's sense of honor.

Humility can at times be thought of as an understated approach to life—being a bit self-deprecating of one's contributions to an event or group. Yet for the leader of a department or organization, being self-deprecating could come off as a sign of weakness—not a quality that someone in a leadership position wants to express. So how do Trustworthy Leaders develop and express humility? By recognizing the importance of others and being of service to them. Humility for a Trustworthy Leader means not letting the trappings of leadership create a swelled head, or sense of importance beyond the role. Humility comes from the rightful acknowledgment of one's own importance to the organization, along with the acknowledgment of everyone else's value as well.

The practice of *reciprocity* follows from a leader's acknowledgment of everyone's value to the organization. Trustworthy Leaders will continue to develop their sense of honor by showing care and respect for the people with whom they work. This caring will be genuine, expressed in efforts to develop balanced, reciprocal relationships with others. A

Trustworthy Leader shows interest in engaging other people in an exchange of ideas and is willing to extend herself and be vulnerable to open up the conversation.

The third quality that contributes to a leader's sense of honor is *position awareness*, which includes awareness of the power that comes from a hierarchical place in the organization and the power that comes from being trustworthy. Power is a force used by people in leadership positions, yet often leaders conflate the power that others assign to the position (position power) and the power that a person actually has at his disposal (personal power). A Trustworthy Leader will be aware of the power assigned to the role and will also have the personal self-awareness necessary to understand the difference between role power and the power to get things done through relationships.

One of the reasons why Trustworthy Leaders are trusted in the first place is because they do not abuse their position power. They are aware of it, they use it for the good of the organization, *and* they have personal power that is stronger than their position power. The strength of their personal power comes from their humility and the reciprocity they practice in their relationships. This trust-based power is much greater than any imputed power that may be assigned to a job title or position on an organization chart.

The three qualities of humility, reciprocity, and position awareness combine to create the overall foundation of honor. And the development of this foundation of honor begins the process of becoming a Trustworthy Leader. Leading with honor serves as a source of continuous replenishment for Trustworthy Leaders throughout their lives. Every moment in which trust can be extended and developed is a reminder of the honor of being a leader.

HUMILITY

Great leaders develop and put into practice the honor they feel in their positions based on a series of life influences and work experiences, with the two often combined. Stew Leonard Sr., the now retired founder of the Connecticut-based regional grocery business that carries his name, rode around in his father's milk truck as a boy, making deliveries and learning the value of good customer service at a very early age. His understanding was further reinforced by a singular incident that happened early in his career, an incident that cemented into place the importance of humility.

As the story is told on the company website, and by Stew himself, a woman who had purchased some eggnog from Stew's original small dairy store (precursor to the Stew Leonard's organization as it exists today) returned it with the complaint that it was sour. Stew's initial reaction was indignation; he didn't sell sour eggnog. He tasted the eggnog that the woman wanted to return and declared it just fine, yet she insisted that it was sour and she wanted her money back. After a quick back-and-forth exchange, Stew ended up pulling out his wallet and reimbursing her right there, yet he lost her as a customer because of his initial challenge to her complaint.

Later that evening, Stew related the incident and his response to his wife, Marianne. Marianne took the customer's point of view, related her own experiences of good and poor customer service, and confirmed that she would have responded exactly the same way—and that she would likely never return to the store as a customer. Well, that of course caused Stew to pause, as he knew that losing customers was not in his best interest. Thinking more broadly, he believed that it was only a very small percentage of people who might intentionally try to mislead a shopkeeper to return an item they had purchased by mistake, and that if he tried to protect himself from the 1 percent who were dishonest, he'd end up penalizing the other 99 percent who were really good and honest.

A physical manifestation of this realization is the Customer Service Rock of Commitment—a huge granite slab that sits at the entrance to every Stew Leonard's store, engraved with the company's two customer service rules. Rule #1 is "THE CUSTOMER IS ALWAYS RIGHT!" Rule #2 is "IF THE CUSTOMER IS EVER WRONG, REREAD RULE #1."

Stew Sr. tells his story with pride now, although at the time it was humbling. It's a singular story that is told often—to all new Team Members, and to everyone who visits a Stew Leonard's store and wants to understand the secrets of their success. And when looked at more deeply, there is a clear connection between this experience of humility that Stew Sr. took so much to heart and the strong Trustworthy Leadership at the company today.

Stew Sr. thought he was right when he first was confronted with the customer who didn't like her eggnog. And he may very well have been right in terms of the quality of the product. Yet it didn't meet the needs of the woman who had purchased it, so for her, it wasn't right. Providing top-quality service to others is dependent on their response to whatever they purchase. Learning how to set aside an initial reaction to hear another person's point of view is an invaluable service lesson, as well as a key step in developing humility.

This value lesson, first experienced by Stew Sr., has been passed on to the four family members in the second generation of the enterprise. Stew Jr. (president and CEO), Jill Tavello (vice president, Culture and Communication), Beth Leonard (executive vice president, responsible for Cheese and Artisan Baking), and Tom Leonard (board member and owner of Tom Leonard's Farmer's Market in Richmond, Virginia) all put into practice the fundamental message that their parents took from this incident: pay attention to the point of view of others, to their comments and concerns, and to how you can meet their needs. By focusing on others, whether they're customers or Team Members, you will be successful at meeting your own goals, and you can create a great workplace in the process. This is a valuable lesson that every aspiring leader would do well to heed.

Stew Jr. and Tavello are both very visible and active in promoting the culture of Stew Leonard's. They talk about their passion for what they do, and they speak of their roles with the same degree of humility as that conveyed by their father. Stew Jr. talks at length about the importance of showing respect to people. One of the ways this occurs, he said, is by making good decisions when no one is looking. He sees this as a sign that leaders are always thinking of others—not just when someone is watching them. He spoke of the importance of having leaders in the stores who are willing to take risks to meet their goals, yet adapt the methods they use to reflect the comfort of their Team Members.

He also spoke of the need to be authentic as a leader, and to be accessible, to never imagine that you are more important than others, and to be cautious about setting things up that might imply that you are a more important person because of your role. "A business consultant was speaking at a luncheon I attended yesterday," he said. "She was talking about promoting leadership training to the C-suite. I didn't even know what the C-suite is. I said I hope there's never a C-suite at Stew Leonard's. You really want a floor-suite where everyone's on the floor." While different people make different contributions to the business, everyone is valuable as a human being, and Stew Jr. wants to make sure that the messages that go out to people convey this clearly.

Stew Jr. is quick to share stories that praise others, telling of a request for help he received from a customer that was ultimately handled by the store workers at the end of a long day: "Last night a customer called me at 9 P.M. She has a kid who needed to go to school dressed as a chef the next day. The outfit they had ordered didn't arrive. I was in New York City at the time, but I told her that I would call the store and arrange for her to pick up an outfit. Well, I forgot to call the store. She came over to the store, though, and asked for the outfit at 10 P.M. Everybody at the store got it together, got her the outfit, and even put a meat thermometer in her sleeve. I didn't even know it had happened. I called her this morning to apologize, and she said, 'No problem! John was fantastic last night.'"

As Stew told this story, he enthused about the performance of his staff, was humbled by their initiative and willingness to pitch in and get things done, and felt very honored to have had a part in creating the workplace culture in which this simple act could happen. Some leaders wouldn't tell this kind of a story—one in which they were asked to help, yet it was others who actually followed through. Some might fear it would show them in a poor light. Yet for Stew, this story exemplified the kind of leadership he *wants* to see at Stew Leonard's: everyone is able to pitch in, and praise for a good act goes to the people who actually provided the service.

This appreciation and credit is communicated freely to Team Members, as I saw firsthand when I toured the flagship store in Norwalk, Connecticut, with Tavello. Tavello introduced me to many of the people who work there, telling me a bit about how long each person had been there and their career histories. She highlighted new product and service ideas—from the meat department to the fruit displays— that Team Members had implemented on their own to meet the needs of customers or to provide new offerings that customers would find enjoyable.

Both Stew Jr. and Tavello spoke of activities and accomplishments that they could have described as their own, or that they could have more closely associated with their own efforts. Yet the examples they used to make their points were all about the accomplishments of others. Their greatness as leaders comes not from the heights to which the two of them have climbed, but from the authenticity with which they speak about everyone in the store. Both Tavello and Stew have been able to pass their philosophy on to others through the stories they tell, their visibility in the stores, the actual physical support they provide to people in need of an extra set of hands, and the praise they provide in public for people's great efforts. All of this reinforces the culture at Stew Leonard's.

As is clear from the Leonards, humility shows itself as an ability to see oneself as part of the process of providing service to people— whether they are customers, patients, suppliers, or shareholders— placing yourself neither above the process nor outside of it. Humility is experienced through the actions of people who practice leadership as supportive rather than threatening, equitable rather than hierarchical. When you are able to share praise and recognition in this way, you will find that benefits will come back to you as well. A *sincere* effort to acknowledge a person's contributions is likely to get you a smile from the recipient and engender a feeling of belonging in that person. Frequent sincere expressions of thanks are one of the most powerful motivators for continued positive actions.

One of the definitions of humility is a willingness to do something out of the goodness of your heart, not for any benefit to yourself. This definition was certainly a large force behind Stew Sr.'s customer service policy. He believed that treating customers and Team Members with respect was, first and foremost, the right thing to do as a human being. Yet this policy also has a strong "business results" underpinning: Stew Leonard's is a very successful business in a highly competitive industry and in a very competitive regional market. Team Members are able to do the right thing for the customer, which creates trust and loyalty, diminishes customer churn, and gives people every reason to expect that the experience of shopping at Stew Leonard's will be enjoyable.

Other than loyal customers, there's another business benefit that comes along with the Customer Is Always Right policy: loyal Team Members. Stew Jr. said his chef costume request was not an unusual one. Customers often ask Team Members for assistance with school projects or special events, and everyone knows that helping them out is a natural part of working at Stew Leonard's, and Team members *enjoy* fulfilling the requests. "It's part of why people like working here," said Stew Jr. "They get information and feel like they are a part of things. And when

---

One of the things I really like about Stew is that he walks the walk. At my last job, my boss had a Stew Leonard's mug on his desk. It showed Rule One and Rule Two. But, that was it. He didn't do anything about it. Here, Stew, he has that rock out front, and he really lives by that. I've seen it countless times. I had a customer come up to me and told me that the bag of apples she had was bad. I said, "Yes, they are bad." I saw that the sticker on the bag was from another store, but I didn't say anything. I just gave her a free bag of apples and gave her money back. I didn't want to embarrass her.

—*A Stew Leonard's Team Member*

they get opportunities to help and share . . . then there is a happy, growing Team Member who is going to stay with you for a while."

RECIPROCITY

Trustworthy Leaders are honored to be in their roles, and they show genuine caring and respect for the people with whom they work. They do this in part by creating balanced, reciprocal relationships. Reciprocity means, on its face, that people in the relationship will experience mutual exchange, the give and take of ideas, sharing of support, and caring for each other's contributions. When we are in a reciprocal relationship we have a duty to share and contribute to the relationship, as well as an obligation to care for what is created by everyone involved. Yet it is one thing to say that you want reciprocity, and quite another to establish true, authentic reciprocity among people in different positions, with different skills and knowledge, and different perceptions of their power. It's a challenge that anyone wanting to become a Trustworthy Leader must take on. Luckily, many examples of how to do this already exist.

Suppose a leader wants to get feedback on an idea he is considering for expanding service in a competitive market. He can send out an email requesting people's comments, or he can get out of his office and go talk with people. In either situation, if the leader is trustworthy, people will know that the request is sincere, unencumbered by strings or hidden agendas, and they will respond. If their responses are cared for—treated with respect, considered thoughtfully, and perhaps partially if not wholly worked into the leader's final decision—then a reciprocal relationship is reinforced. Interactions based in respect create room for discussion and allow for challenges on a variety of topics. No one gets in trouble for poking holes in an idea, nor is anyone resented for presenting a variation on the idea that's even stronger. A Trustworthy Leader will show a genuine interest in engaging people in an exchange, as well as a willingness to extend himself, to be vulnerable, in order to level the playing field. Trust and reciprocity of this caliber do not happen overnight, but rather are built over time.

For people to begin to develop mutual trust, one person in the relationship needs to take the initiative and start the process. In situations in which there are differences in power, responsibility, access to resources, and control over resources, it is generally the person with more of those designations who needs to begin. Taking the initiative can be as simple as starting a conversation, stopping by for an impromptu visit, or ensuring that a promise—for training, for support, for the answer to a question—is actually fulfilled. These first steps set the stage and level the playing field, giving the person with less power or status an opportunity to participate in the conversation without having started from the more vulnerable place of being first. Looked at from another side, when a leader is willing to extend an offer, he becomes a bit more exposed in the relationship. Something is offered, which the other person can accept or reject, and both of those reactions will have a personal impact on the one who started things off. This opening can help a person with less power, or different resources, feel more comfortable in testing the waters that can lead to mutual trust and true reciprocity.

A great example of this cycle of initiation and response comes from Chris Van Gorder, who for the past eleven years has been the CEO of Scripps Health. He has also championed a major turnaround within the Scripps system. During our interviews, Van Gorder spoke of the sense of honor that he experiences in his work, primarily by describing the ways in which others, especially the frontline staff, give their best to the organization every day. Yet within his stories are examples of his own actions that began the turnaround process, in which he extended himself to others to get things started, creating a pattern of reciprocity that continues to support the organization today.

Van Gorder came on as CEO during a tumultuous time, with votes of no confidence in previous leaders, financial problems with no end in sight, and staffing problems resulting from the poor culture that existed at the hospitals. Yet there was also hope and the possibility for change.

Right off, Van Gorder noticed the quality of the people who worked at Scripps. "You could tell they were frustrated and angry and embarrassed," he said, "but there were good people here. I think you will find good, caring people at any health care organization, as the field draws that kind of person.

"I had been around long enough," he continued, "and I had enough education—experience more than anything—to say 'I can't change the culture by myself.' I mean, I could demonstrate certain behaviors, but in a big organization with multiple sites that's not enough. And I can't just write a memo saying the culture will change. So I said, 'You know what? We are going to have to do it slowly, and maybe not even finish it during my tenure here at Scripps.'"

A leader with a less developed sense of honor might have approached the situation differently. A leader with a sense of entitlement might have felt compelled to solve the problems on his own, or to solve the pieces of it that would show improvement on paper and look the best on his own record. But Van Gorder, honored by the position he held and fully aware of the responsibility that it entailed, began the process of change by practicing reciprocity. Namely, Van Gorder created the Scripps Leadership Academy, a leadership development program that started with three people from each hospital site joining each other—and Van Gorder himself—on a journey to remake Scripps.

He described his change initiative as a systemic process in which he, as the leader who had the responsibility, resources, and power to start the process, would take the first step. And his first step was to invite others into the culture change process and let them know that he believed that they were the ones who would actually be making the changes in the culture at Scripps. He took himself out of the picture as the most important person by making a public commitment that the Leadership Academy, and all of its participants, would lead the way in changing the culture at Scripps.

"Initially," Van Gorder said, "some of the candidates that applied and were accepted were not the top people from each site. Most of the top people thought this was going to be Management 101 and that they were already good managers, so they didn't need it." However, there were enough people willing to accept Van Gorder's offer, and the program began. When leaders initiate culture change processes, some can get discouraged if they put themselves out there only to find their own enthusiasm isn't matched by everyone else in the organization. Yet Van Gorder knew that change *had* to happen, and he was committed to starting with those people who were willing to go forward.

In the first session of the first class, a lively question-and-answer session with Van Gorder ensued. As long as the questions wouldn't violate an employee's rights or infringe on a confidentiality agreement, Van Gorder said he would answer anything—and the questions kept coming in that first session, for over two and a half hours. And he answered them all. "I told people that I wanted them to learn how to ask questions," he said, "that I would chide them for not asking tough questions." We'll address the importance of sharing information more fully in Chapter Five; for now, simply note that with both Van Gorder's invitation to participate and the way in which he let himself be subject to questioning, he began a cycle of true, authentic reciprocity.

The first open-ended question-and-answer session was such a success that it became a mainstay of every subsequent Leadership Academy class. Van Gorder also gave participants an assignment: a team-based project to tackle a pressing issue facing the organization as a whole. Participants were talking, and they were acting.

A cynical observer of the Leadership Academy might claim that this effort was simply a way to get people to believe that they could make changes, when in reality the senior leaders would do what they wanted to do, regardless. A skeptic might suspect that the Academy was a way of shirking responsibility and shifting the heavy burden of changing the culture onto other people's shoulders. Van Gorder acknowledged that these comments, and others, were made when things first got started. But no one's saying it now.

The financial and structural health of Scripps has changed dramatically, in part because of the success of the Leadership Academy and people's participation in the change process. Between 2002 and 2010,

Scripps profits more than tripled, increasing from $27 million to $237 million. Key industry business metrics, like Days Cash on Hand, also improved. (Quite literally, this refers to the average number of days it takes to deplete a business's supply of cash.) Scripps' Days Cash on Hand more than doubled, from 72 to 205, putting them in a much stronger financial position. Scripps has emerged from this first long part of their change process in a position of tremendous strength. And a big part of the reason is that Van Gorder didn't just ask for input. He invited people in, listened to their ideas, and acted—with them.

"At the end of the first year," Van Gorder said, "I got a question from one of the [Leadership Academy] participants. He said, 'Now what? We've had a year with you. We trust you, but what's next?'" The trust itself was a huge step forward from where Scripps had been and an important foundational piece. But the question—What next?—was an apt one. It was time to tackle some more deeply entrenched dilemmas that were affecting the overall success of the organization. Van Gorder asked each class participant to do two things: to deliver more to the people who worked for them, and to ask more of those same people. And he asked the participants to demand more from *him*, to challenge him with questions about problems or opportunities that could be taken on. He firmly believed that now that he had a team of leaders in place with whom there was a reciprocal trust-based relationship, many of the dilemmas at Scripps could be solved if they were brought to his attention and taken on by everyone.

Each subsequent class in the Leadership Academy experienced the same kind of teaching style—plenty of opportunities for questions and answers, and an assignment to complete a team-based project that would address some pressing issue. Each class received the same invitation to participate in a reciprocal trust-based relationship. None of this would have been successful if trust had been broken. The fact that the Leadership Academy has continued—with a new class every year since 2000—and Scripps has grown and improved significantly, is testimony to the success of this culture change process. It took years to accomplish. And it has taken a great deal of investment on the part of leaders—

starting with Van Gorder, and involving everyone who is leading in some capacity at Scripps.

The Scripps story offers a wonderful example of how an individual leader who experiences his role as an honor can approach a daunting task, and engage others in the process of reenergizing a culture. Van Gorder's efforts provide two key take-away messages about how to create a process that will work, beyond the fundamental need to practice reciprocity. Van Gorder took time. He actually assumed that he might not be around for the full culture change process to finish. He also created an opportunity for people to experience what he wanted them eventually to put into practice.

As you seek to become a Trustworthy Leader, taking the time to develop your skills and abilities is essential. Developing trust is not something to be rushed. And creating opportunities for people to experience the hoped-for long-term outcome will develop an anticipation of what could be, serving as an incentive for people to continue with their efforts. The first class in the Leadership Academy became a word-of-mouth marketing campaign for the ongoing change efforts at Scripps. Creating that type of an experience for people in your own organization will be equally valuable.

> There are so many things that make Scripps great, but the one that stands out for the employees is the way that Chris Van Gorder communicates with us. His leadership is incredible, and he takes the time to teach classes in CPR, first aid, etc. to his employees. He displays respect for his employees regardless of race, gender, or age, and they give it back. He is a true example of a great leader, and it would be a sad day for Scripps Health if he ever decided to retire.
>
> —*Scripps employee*

POSITION AWARENESS

Position awareness, the third part of developing your sense of honor, does not mean you are aware that you are a program director, vice president, or project manager. The title on your business card will fulfill that requirement! Rather, position awareness means that you know where you fit within a group of people, and you are comfortable with that place. You recognize the role that you hold within the flow of activity and information in a department, a division, or the organization as a whole. With position awareness, you have an understanding of the distribution networks tied to your position and the departments and people you can rely on to get things done.

For Trustworthy Leaders who need to rely on many people, position awareness can be a tremendous asset. Leaders who are successful in understanding where and how they fit will enhance their power and effectiveness because they will be able to rely on their trust-based relationships with others to help them get things done—just as we saw with Chris Van Gorder. These leaders will receive valuable information from people they are in touch with and can pass that information on to others to enhance their success.

In contrast, leaders who do not have strong position awareness are likely to constrict the value of information and opportunities that flow into and out from their positions. This can happen because of their sense that they are more important than others and so "deserve" more than their fair share, or more than what is equitable. Poor position awareness is also evident when people are insecure about their own worth relative to others. Much like the title character in *The Wizard of Oz*, insecure leaders cloak themselves in the mythology of their power, rather than developing power through their trust-based relationships.

Position awareness combines awareness of the power that is available simply because of the position one holds (position power), and the power that comes with being self-aware and respectful of others (personal power). Trustworthy Leaders are aware of these two forms of power that affect organizational life, and they also hold an appreciation for how things can most effectively get done with other people's willing participation. While some leaders rely almost completely on their position power to get things done, Trustworthy Leaders place greater emphasis on their personal power. They know that using personal power that contains humility and a stance of reciprocity will be more effective.

When a leader has position awareness, she does not need to participate in games and politicking. She doesn't take credit for an idea that wasn't hers, or hint that she has information she can't share because of the discrepancy between her position power and yours. When politicking is absent, something far more productive takes its place: a collegial environment, one in which people feel comfortable seeking and sharing ideas regardless of their job title. So a sales clerk who is widely considered to be clear-headed and sharp might be consulted by the marketing director on an issue that is far removed from both the responsibilities in his job description and the power assigned to the sales clerk position on an organization chart. In this case, successful position awareness helps to remove any need to pay attention to the organization chart altogether; as a result, the marketing director gains access to valuable insights that could positively influence a business decision.

Certainly there are people in specific roles who hold ultimate responsibility for making decisions. Leaders with great position awareness don't diminish their authority in those cases in which a decision appropriate to the role must be made and implemented. Stew Leonard Jr. and Chris Van Gorder, to use just two examples, are strong, determined leaders willing and able to make tough decisions when they need to. And their decisions are successfully implemented because of the respect with which they interact with others. When a company has a history of power being shared rather than hoarded, then at the time of tough decision-making sessions, leaders can be assured that relationships will stay strong—no matter how difficult the topic or significant the decision.

To more fully explore this concept, we return to REI's Sally Jewell and see an excellent example of the importance of position awareness in a leader's process of becoming trustworthy. Jewell shows genuine interest in the lives of others, sees the leadership role itself as honorable, and creates the conditions in which she herself experiences honor.

"I have found that the farther away I get from my position in the organizational hierarchy, the more open people are with me," she said. "I will be much more likely to get really good feedback about whether or not what we're saying is trustworthy or, frankly, whether the message we're trying to convey is making it down throughout the organization. The feedback I get from my conversations with people is anecdotal, it's subjective, but it is more important to me than the objective data because it validates whether something is real or not.

"As a CEO," she acknowledged, "it can be difficult to always get honest, thoughtful feedback because you've got position power and people are intimidated by the position, even if you try to make it easy. Yet when I'm visiting one of the stores, and I put on a green vest and am fumbling through answering a question, and I call in an expert who knows more than I do, that speaks volumes. Or when I put on a green vest and I actually sell a kayak and a paddle to a person who didn't even know they came in to buy a kayak, that also sends a message: that I can speak from personal experience and share an enthusiasm for what others are doing at REI. The message will become so much broader than that one person or that one story. It gets to be viral and is authentic."

What goes viral and gets shared from employee to employee, store to store, is the story about how the CEO sold someone a kayak, and asked for help from one of the in-store experts, as well as the fact that she got to work by putting on the green vest and stepping into someone else's role. When leaders in an organization move out from the trappings of their position, they are stepping away from their position power. When you don the clothing of others—like the green vest—it signals that you are putting yourself into another position, one in which your own accumulated power and knowledge may be less than that of the people who are actively serving in that position. And when you ask for help from an expert in sales, thus acknowledging that the expert knows more than you about how to handle something, that is a significant sign of respect for the sales position and the person who usually holds it.

> Some members of my team delivered excellent customer service to a father and his autistic son. Well, the father mentioned his experience on a blog. People at headquarters up to the CEO heard and read the blog. The CEO herself, Sally Jewell, sent me an email and a personal note to my employees thanking them. That level of recognition for the daily efforts of employees is unfounded in the retail environment. It shows the investment and understanding that the executives in the corporation have for the employees. At REI, people really do care.
>
> —*REI store employee*

All of these actions that involve a step away from position power will actually bring you closer to the personal power that is so vital to your success as a leader. Jewell's actions contribute to a sense of equity among people at REI—a sense that, under a different leader, might not exist. Leaders can foster this type of down-to-earth culture well, or they can do it poorly. Jewell does it well because it's authentic—she has great respect for the people in her organization and the work that they do, and she feels honored to serve as their CEO.

Jewell strives to lead REI so that everyone is able to be personally successful—within their positions, within groups, and as members of the organization. People are given responsibilities, provided with training to help them fulfill their responsibilities, and treated with respect that conveys their value as people, not just as employees. This whole dynamic creates an excitement that you can feel when you talk with people. They are excited about what they are doing, in part because it holds value. And they know this because others tell them, be they colleagues, leaders, customers, or co-op members. Everyone at REI is supported in the development of position awareness. They are encouraged to see their position power as something they can minimize and to develop their personal power, which they are encouraged to strengthen. This is one of the ways in which each person at REI knows that they are important to the success of the organization. This strategy and approach to power is developed and shared throughout the organization, so everyone can feel the honor inherent in their positions and the contributions they make.

Erin Hass, who has been with REI for fifteen years and now leads the training and development function there, spoke of the very intentional ways in which she seeks to help people understand and use their personal power. Sometimes it involves challenging people to figure out the logistics of a project themselves, once she's given them general guidance. Stephanie Fischer, a senior training and development specialist on Hass's team, may struggle initially as she relies on her personal power to collaborate on the design and implementation of a training program, yet she will become a better teacher of the concept when called on to do so. "Erin stays engaged with the team while we are working on design," says Fischer, "yet she's not involved in every meeting. She never loses sight of what's going on within our function and with us personally. I'm doing most of the work, but she's always engaged in that process with me."

Hass's goal is to help people learn the benefits of involving others based on their own experience of needing to ask for help to get their own projects completed. As she sees it, the work of the training and development department should echo REI's broad commitment to service. "REI is here to serve our members, and as a leader, you're here to serve the employees that work with you. It's a situation where you're involving others in decisions—always."

Jewell herself has established a requirement for volunteer service—on a board of directors or in a community-based organization—as part of the developmental work she asks of the REI executive team. As Hass described it, "For her, when you're serving on a board, you're learning how to be a leader without position power. When you're a VP, senior VP, executive VP, you've got quite a bit of position power, and people will just do things because you say to do them, not necessarily because they want to." The volunteer experience thus gives executives an awareness of different types of power. Hass continued, "Sally really wants to make sure that people understand how to get things done without position power."

There is much that can be assumed when one is in a position with the title of manager, director, or president, yet assumed power does not always hold up to the test of use if relationships with colleagues are weak and based on expectations of compliance versus trust. When employees are told to do something by leaders who have assumed the power they believe should be associated with their position, employees may comply with the request to complete the task, yet go no further. This is not to deny the reality of job requirements, yet these can be met at the same time that more is offered; namely with the discretionary effort so many leaders want from their employees.

REI is the most unique company I have ever known. I've never known a company to treat their employees the way they do. It's great. They're wonderful. It's such a pleasant place to work in. The people are so friendly and supportive. They treat you with respect and offer assistance whenever you need it. Management works with employees to make the workplace as stress-free as possible. I was fortunate to meet the CEO of REI, Sally Jewell. It was the first time I ever had a CEO shake my hand and treat me like an equal. She's great!
—REI employee

CONTINUING THE CIRCLE

In the examples provided throughout this chapter, we can see that Patrick Charmel, Stew Leonard Jr., Chris Van Gorder, and Sally Jewell have all developed their sense of the honor of leadership. They each understand the power that they have access to through the positions they hold. They also understand that to act honorably in their roles means to use their power in the best interests of those people who are dependent on their sound judgment.

Power is not used to manipulate people, nor is it used to gain more for yourself at the expense of others. True power comes from what others give to you in a reciprocal relationship, not from what you take.

Reciprocity depends on your humility to not see yourself as more or less valuable than others, to be able to acknowledge people's rightful value to the organization. Understanding all of this puts you on the path to creating a Virtuous Circle and developing a sense of the honor that will come with being a Trustworthy Leader.

Our focus on the honor of leadership has touched on the deeply held personal values that guide leaders' interactions with and service to others. Woven throughout each story has also been an undercurrent of the next element on the Trustworthy Leader's journey: the idea of inclusion. As with every step along the way, one element of the Trustworthy Leader's journey will lead into the next.

Uncovering the Roots of Honor

A sense of honor is the starting point in a leader's movement through the Virtuous Circle, so there is great value in being able to recognize the various experiences and life lessons that have instilled Trustworthy Leaders with their sense of honor. Where exactly does it start? What triggers the search to understand what it means to be honored and to act with honor—to fully explore humility, reciprocity, and position awareness? While the answer will be different for every great leader, understanding even one person's background can help us see just how deeply rooted the development of honor is, and it can encourage us to look for the life lessons that have influenced our own personal sense of honor.

Chris Van Gorder of Scripps tells a compelling story about a particular event that served as a starting place for the development of his sense of honor. A large part of Van Gorder's approach to leadership is a system of exchange that honors the gifts that people bring to the workplace. In Van Gorder's case, he learned about the importance of qualities such as humility, reciprocity, and position awareness not through their presence in his early working life, but through their absence.

Van Gorder started his career as a police officer, yet left that role due to an on-the-job injury. He began his health care career as an emergency room clerk and then became a security guard (not at Scripps), working night shifts to support himself as he went through school. One night as he was doing his rounds, he happened to notice that the hospital administrator was walking down the hall toward him, perhaps returning from a meeting.

"I was about as low on the totem pole as you can be in my position," Van Gorder remembered, "and I saw the hospital administrator, recognized him by his photograph, and he's walking down in the basement in the middle of the night. And I went, 'Wow—I am going to get a shot at meeting this guy.' And I will never forget what happened.

"He walked by me as if I didn't even exist.

"There was nobody else there, and I remember how crushed I felt that the guy didn't even acknowledge me as he walked by. I thought about it and thought, you know what, that's not right. Because if anything bad happens in this hospital right now, they are going to call me before they call him. Everyone has their role and their purpose in life, and sometimes, in fact most times, the people who are out there in the field doing good work are far more important than I will ever be in my position now as CEO. And so I always try to treat people well so that they know how much I respect their hard work."

What Van Gorder experienced in that moment in the hallway is unfortunately something that many working people experience on a daily basis—an oblivious lack of recognition on the part of an organizational leader that conveys to you that you don't exist in that leader's world. And it sets in motion a reciprocal exchange that many leaders claim not to want: an exchange based in mistrust and skepticism. Yet how can you be expected to honor and respect a leader who has just walked by you, acting as if you don't exist?

It would probably surprise that hospital administrator to know that his act of walking past Van Gorder that night with no acknowledgment is still remembered. Not just remembered, actually, but the basis for the dramatically different style of leadership that exists at Scripps Health. This is a powerful example of the small actions that can have huge impacts. Luckily for the people at Scripps, the impact of this incident has been very positive. With this brief encounter as a starting point, Van Gorder has developed an honorable approach to leadership that has earned him, Scripps Health, and Scripps employees tremendous positive recognition for their professional accomplishments—and financial stability for the entire organization.

CHAPTER THREE

INCLUSION

Discussions about inclusion may be familiar to you. We hear a lot about it in reference to our education system, when teachers, parents, and administrators talk about the importance of mainstreaming kids into classrooms. You may hear about the need for inclusion after ethnic tension arises in a community. And inclusion has more recently become a familiar topic in the workplace, as part of an effort to move beyond initial conversations about diversity into the realm of collaboration and cooperation.

In great workplaces, inclusion reflects a desire to see beyond visible differences to the tremendous similarities that exist among people. Many organizations have tapped into this idea by helping people to explore their similarities and differences that are *not* visible, but that are instead discovered through conversation and interaction. In essence, a great workplace can be seen as a giant diversity network in the making, with people seeking to connect with each other across barriers, real or imagined.

Inclusion begins with a leader's invitation to everyone to join the organization on equal terms. The stated goals of many diversity programs and the positive aspirations of many inclusion programs are similar: to create a workplace environment in which people can work together and be successful. Yet different approaches to inviting people in can have very different consequences. Take, for example, the following stories from IBM and TDIndustries.

During the 1970s and '80s, IBM was known as a very successful technology company dominating the market with its mainframe computers. IBM employees were often characterized as "suits," due to the strict dress code that existed for virtually everyone: a dark gray or blue suit, white shirt, and "sincere" tie. Facial hair was discouraged, if not completely forbidden, and haircuts needed to be neat and short. For women entering IBM's ranks, conservative suits and ties were also expected, and a new cottage industry developed, trying to teach women how to dress for success so that they could fit in as much as possible. Fitting in meant trying to look similar to the people already there.

This cultural strategy of creating a workforce in which people "fit in" was part of a marketing and sales strategy meant to convey confidence to potential customers. Big Blue would always be there for you, no matter which individual happened to be your contact person. Yet for the employees trying to "fit in," the Big Blue identity came at a steep cost: their individuality and all of the creativity that might come with it was suppressed. IBM, known for being a caring if somewhat homogenous organization, went through wrenching times as technology and culture changes moved through the economy in the late '80s and early '90s. The company had difficulty adapting quickly and at times seemed to be two steps behind competitors.

The iconic image of the "suit" culture became symbolic of many organizations in similar situations that were unable to adapt to cultural and economic shifts. A homogenous culture, in which one look, one set of ideas, and one approach to business was the norm, steered many companies into a wall. IBM righted itself and has taken on a strong stance for the future based on promoting and valuing diversity, seeking to shed the "suit" imagery that was an overlay on the company's culture for so long.

A second organization started with a different approach. TDIndustries, long recognized as a great workplace, began with a foundation of valuing diversity. Jack Lowe Sr., the company founder, played an integral role in desegregating the Dallas, Texas, public school system in the 1960s, and he brought his personal values into the organization. He often stated that the differences among people were actually some of the greatest strengths of the company. "Valuing individual differences" is one of TD's basic values, and programs have always been in place to help people work well with each other, regardless of their backgrounds.

As an example, TD has regularly provided English language instruction to their non-English-speaking partners (all employees are owners of the company, thus the term *partners* is used). This practice stems from a deeper belief that "good communication leads to understanding between people" and that barriers to communication can often occur among people who are not fluent in each other's languages. TD could have stopped here with its language program, yet that would be a one-sided approach to inclusion that would in some ways hark back to a homogenous "suits" culture. Yet without really giving it much thought, TD went further.

TD offers Spanish classes to its English-speaking partners as an initiative to further overcome communication barriers. Study materials for key programs such as Catch the Spirit, Safety Orientation, Benefit Orientation, and Leadership Development are offered in both English and Spanish. All partner benefits information is presented in English and Spanish. The *TDSpirit* newsletter includes a bilingual message from the CEO. And a Spanish-language version of the TDCulture video has been created so that all partners are given the opportunity to understand the scope of TD's mission and basic values.

All of these efforts, and many, many more, reflect a commitment to valuing diversity and promoting inclusion in ways that enable people to come to the workplace as distinct individuals. Everyone is invited into the culture of TDIndustries and asked to join with the mission and values of the organization just as they are, with no need for any homogenizing.

One of the key reasons that inclusive workplace programs such as those implemented by TDIndustries, IBM, and other companies are successful is that their leaders themselves are comfortable with people's differences. Leaders who have genuinely expressed their own commitment to inclusion—and show their comfort with differences through their actions and words—create inclusive environments that are supportive of others. Creating an inclusive environment can be a challenge in some organizations if the people in leadership positions look and act more like one another than like the broad expanse of people employed in their organizations. Yet it is not impossible.

Leaders who want to create a culture of inclusion at their company *can* do so. In fact, that's an important part of creating a great workplace and being a Trustworthy Leader. Trustworthy Leaders seek to include people and their differences and to support the development of cross-group connections that help people share their distinct approaches and ideas. Many have challenged themselves to expand their notions of who fits in what type of position, and who might be able to come up with "the brilliant idea" that will advance the company. They are willing to take bold steps to explore their personal prejudices and the limitations of cultural norms and expectations.

Some ways in which leaders create cross-group connections are fairly common: through networking and affinity groups. Others are subtle. Leaders who are comfortable with and connected to many different people throughout the organization can use the physical environment to help people from different areas to meet—for example, through the simple act of eating lunch in an open setting and inviting people to join them at the table. Visiting people in different departments and taking colleagues along also breaks down barriers, as does assigning people to cross-department project teams. Moving into a different space to get work done can be unsettling initially, yet the strong connection that everyone has with the Trustworthy Leader provides support and comfort, weakening preestablished group boundaries so that new connections can flourish.

An ability to be comfortable with people who appear to be different from you is very helpful in a variety of work situations. Comfort with others can ease the strain of workplace transfers and enable people to move quickly into new positions. It can also enliven discussions, as the hesitation that often comes with discomfort will be diminished and conversations will be richer. And from a leader's perspective, the sooner that people are comfortable with each other, the sooner they will be able to collaborate, share ideas, and provide great service to each other and to customers.

A leader's ability to be inclusive and to create a culture of inclusion in the workplace is a strategic necessity in our increasingly inter-connected world. A variety of people have made the case for the benefits that come from inclusion and diversity, including Robert Putnam, a professor of public policy at Harvard University. He states that ethnic diversity is inevitable, desirable, and beneficial—and a tremendous social asset that communities, including organizations, should seek to foster. He explains that, although increased diversity may initially lead people to close ranks, when people are brought together in a trusting environment their social networks will expand, as will their comfort with people who are visibly different from them. His studies affirm that enhanced creativity is one of the many benefits of a diverse community, which is in turn associated with more rapid economic growth.[1]

Another person making a strong case for the benefits of diversity is University of Michigan professor Scott Page. In his book *The Difference*, he provides incontrovertible evidence that over time diverse groups of people make better decisions than individuals or homogenous groups, no matter how brilliant the individual or homogenous group members may be. Page provides both narrative explanations that support his findings as well as reams of statistical evidence to add further weight to his conclusion—that there is tremendous value in diversity. As he says, "A talented 'I' and a talented 'they' can become an even more talented 'we.'"[2]

The evidence from Putnam's and Page's research affirms my own findings as well. In 2007 I began looking at the experiences of employees in the 100 Best Companies and comparing their responses on an extensive employee survey with those of employees in the companies that applied to be one of the 100 Best, yet weren't selected. What I confirmed is that among the 100 Best Companies, employees with different visible characteristics—age, race, and gender—had experiences that were more positive and more similar to each other's than did employees in the non-Best companies.[3] This means that a forty-five-year-old African American woman and a thirty-five-year-old Caucasian male in a 100 Best Company were more likely to be experiencing a similar level of management credibility, personal and professional respect, and organizational fairness than would those same employees in a non-Best company.

What is even more striking is the similarity of experiences that people in Best Companies have when considered by job type. We often assume that an hourly employee—who is typically in a position that comes with weaker job security, lower wages, less control over the time and place of work, and so on—will not have the same positive experience of work as will a salaried employee. Yet among employees at the 100 Best Companies, hourly and salaried employees indicated strikingly similar positive perceptions of their work experiences. Why? Because everyone who works in a great workplace—which the 100 Best exemplify—is invited into the organization by their Trustworthy Leaders and helped to become a full member. Their various talents are uncovered and exploited, and a great workplace is created that is financially successful, able to attract and retain the best people, and able to provide products and services that attract and retain customers.

What motivates leaders in great companies to create inclusive environments that are open and welcoming to lots of different kinds of people? Do they anticipate the tremendous benefits their businesses will receive, as well as the positive shift that happens for the people who work there? The answers to these questions are complex, as is the development of an inclusive culture. The ability to promote inclusion comes from a person's deeply held belief in the value of others, a willingness to look for ideas outside of one's own group, and a belief that the benefits that are given to one group of people should be broadened and shared fairly with all. This is what the second element in the Virtuous Circle of the Trustworthy Leader is all about.

GENUINE BELIEF IN THE VALUE OF OTHERS

I have often said that there is no group of people—based on age, race, gender, orientation, height, weight, ability, or any other characteristic—that has a lock on brilliance. Many others have said the same thing. Yet not nearly as many people are willing to *act* on their belief that brilliance is present across all the differences that combine to create human beings. This leads to the reality in some organizations that the differences that people bring to the table can end up being reasons to exclude.

Trustworthy Leaders in great workplaces are willing to take action, to seek out everyone's brilliance, ideas, and contributions, yet still they face challenges. A lifetime's experience of homogeneity can make it difficult to be comfortable around people who are different from you, much less to actively seek them out. If what you've done for most of your life has tended to place you within a certain group of people who look, think, and act in ways similar to you—how do you move beyond that?

At Perkins Coie, a Seattle-based regional law firm headed to national and international prominence, there is ample evidence that it is possible for a small group of homogenous leaders to move beyond tradition-bound roots to create an inclusive culture. Simply put, Perkins Coie is committed to ensuring that their legal skills are their top competitive advantage. Their goal is to find, recruit, and retain the most brilliant employees, and the best way to do this is to seek this talent in *all* corners of the human landscape. Their commitment to quality—and an openness among senior partners to find the best lawyers, wherever and whoever they may be—has led to some remarkable practices in a professional industry not known for its cutting-edge diversity and inclusion practices. At Perkins Coie, leaders start with the genuineness of their interest—in bringing the best people in to work at the firm, in creating an environment in which they can thrive, and in being open to critiques and challenges to ensure that this really happens.

Bob Giles, managing partner of Perkins Coie, and Craig Courter, COO, represent the traditional race and gender categories that people associate with the legal profession. Yet they are both notable for their commitment to inclusion and their willingness to take action. Courter said that among the reasons he came to Perkins Coie were the people he met and their emphasis on quality. "We have excellent lawyers and staff. . . . On occasion a client might look at us in an area and say, 'You don't have the resources to staff this matter,' but they never look at us and say, 'You don't have the quality of lawyers.' We have unbelievable quality in the practices that we have. I like that, and I think that's really important. You can have other strategies to be successful, I'm not saying you can't. Yet we've chosen quality."

If we ended the conversation about value with Courter's statement, we would be covering only half of the issue, for it's not enough to just bring the best in; you have to make sure to foster an environment in which everyone can bring their gifts to the table. You need to recognize the value and quality in a diverse workforce, and you need to make sure you are able to harness that talent.

"I think that one would be hard-pressed in this day and age to find anyone at a firm of the caliber of Perkins Coie who would say that promoting diversity and inclusion in the legal profession is a bad idea," said Linda Walton, the chair of the firm's Strategic Diversity committee.[4] "In fact, most lawyers would tell you that because a truly diverse and inclusive firm delivers far better service to its clients, the promotion of diversity and inclusion is, in fact, a very good idea. Unfortunately, many a good idea in this world has never come to fruition because of a loss of momentum after a glorious inception." Fortunately for Perkins Coie, their leadership has not lost momentum; they have followed through, in ways large and small, and facilitated an environment in which their employees can be themselves, and the firm is very successful.

A number of the Perkins Coie associates I talked with during a focus group spoke of their initial experience starting to work there, and they confirmed that even within the normal challenges of being a new associate at a fast-paced, high-powered law firm, they felt valued and included.

Alvaro Alvarez, an associate with Perkins Coie since 2003, said, "I'd never heard of Perkins Coie before they came out to recruit at Michigan. They seemed genuinely friendly—not just interview friendly—and very interested in creating a diverse group of employees. So I came out for the summer, and I found out that they were very committed to diversity. And nine years later I still see that, and it's important to me."

Other associates talked about the support they received on moving to Seattle from their more diverse origins. "My impression when I got to Seattle was like 'Where are all the brown people?'" said one person. "Yet when you get into the firm, they have all this support— diversity committees and support groups and affinity groups." At first, she thought all of the various groups were a bit much, but then she came to see it differently. The firm understood Seattle's limitations, as far as being a relatively homogenous city. And the firm was making a sincere effort to understand how that might affect someone coming from a different, more diverse setting, and to remedy it. "If I was in New York," she continued, "I wouldn't need to have a destination meeting point to find other people who look like me. I think what Perkins is doing is really important—they want diversity, they recognize the city they're in, and so they want people to feel comfortable. Part of helping with the initial transition is being able to be with people who are like you and who look like you. It's nice to not feel alone at first. It feels a little contrived, but it works—it's really been helpful."

One of the reasons that more employees are fully engaged—with their hearts *and* minds—at great companies like Perkins Coie is that formal and informal support networks create strong internal ties among those who may be seen as different or who may hold positions traditionally seen as having different status or value. These networks create a sense of belonging for people who may not usually feel like part of the group, and they provide an opening for people to share their ideas when they may not initially have the confidence to speak up. Diversity networks and collaborative groups can also serve as resource networks that expose executives or senior managers (who may be a more homogenous group) to people, sources of information, and ideas that are different from their own. These networks can also help those executives understand why it may be difficult for people who are "different" to feel comfortable in some business settings. Participants are emboldened to contribute, without losing their valuable different way of looking at things.

When new recruits at Perkins Coie become members of the team, they have access to firm leaders and are introduced to clients simply as "my colleague"—not "my associate" or "junior associate." These simple acts of inclusion have had a tremendous impact on some of the newer associates, who commented about the difference between their experiences at Perkins Coie and those they have heard about from their friends at other law firms. "We have access to the leaders of the firm because they show up at events," said one. "We get to meet them, and we talk about cases and issues."

No one is wearing rose-colored glasses, though. The associates understand that they are at Perkins Coie because they meet the central criteria: they fall into the "unbelievable quality" category. They also know that their particular perspective, which has been influenced by who they are and their unique experiences, is genuinely valued. Associates were frank about the fact that the work is challenging and hours are

> I have always been impressed with the diversity of the firm—not just ethnic or gender diversity, which thrive, but also diversity of backgrounds, points of view, and particular strengths. This makes the firm an extraordinarily rich and enjoyable place to work.
> —*Associate, Perkins Coie*

long. Yet everyone understood that they were there because of the quality of their skills and ability to contribute, and that made everyone feel included and valued.

ACTIVELY SEEKING OTHERS' IDEAS

Once a great group of people have been invited into an organization and its culture, it is important to get them to stay, and to take advantage of both the incredible talent they brought with them and the potential growth they will pursue during their career. What will keep people, and what leaders need to pursue as the next step in the inclusion process, is to create an environment in which people's ideas are actively sought.

General Mills is a company with a long history. Its roots go back to two flour mills that were built on the banks of the Mississippi in 1866. While the company has always been involved in food production, there were years when other products were a part of the General Mills portfolio. Yet in the recent past, the company has returned to its primary focus on food products and has continued to be very successful. And at General Mills, as at Perkins Coie, a diverse group of people has been genuinely invited into the business and, through various mechanisms, their ideas are actively sought out.

In my discussions with leaders and employees alike at General Mills, one consistent thread that ran throughout all the stories was a focus on solving problems or pursuing opportunities by seeking new ideas and trying new approaches. Chairman and CEO Ken Powell said that one of the reasons he came to General Mills after business school was because he wanted the opportunity to contribute that General Mills espoused; he wanted to actually have a voice in solving problems and finding a new approach. "I was at Stanford business school, and I was clear that I wanted to be hands-on and run and lead something that was real," he said. "So I came out here, and I loved the people I met, I liked the brands, and I felt like I was going to get to run something and have an impact here pretty early.

"I came in as a marketing assistant, and I was the only guy from California, and I had a beard," Powell recalled of his early days, "so I was the marketing assistant on Nature Valley Granola—a little bit of typecasting. I did that, yet right away I was also given opportunities, and for me, that's where we are very different as a company. My next product was to help produce, distribute, and sell Yoplait. That was a great experience, completely different, with a small team, very self-contained. We made mistakes and learned a lot on the way. . . . Even going back to when the company was smaller, I think one of the approaches here was to do different things because that's how you learn. People were very flexible—however you want to do it." Powell's ideas were actively sought, and he was given the chance to implement the ideas himself. The lessons he took from this experience are reflected in his own practice of inclusion as a leader and in the commitment to openness he encourages all leaders to practice through-out General Mills.

Many of the employees with whom I talked expressed a sentiment similar to Powell's. They were attracted to General Mills because they felt it was a place where they could have a voice, and they've been given the same access to opportunities. "I work in HR now, and I started my career here in marketing," said one employee. "I think what I've seen about General Mills is that we genuinely value people, that we value each other. Having worked at other companies, that's something very special, and that's one of the reasons I've stayed."

"For me," said another employee, "what's great is the culture of collaborative teamwork that manifests itself in many different ways. One way is that people look beyond their functions, so the finance analyst doesn't think of herself as just a finance analyst, but when she sees the marketing decisions going awry, she'll speak up in a productive way. People think beyond their roles for the good of the business. Another way we see collaborative teamwork is just in very creative problem solving—bouncing ideas off each other."

A huge piece of fostering this environment where ideas are actively sought is mentorship. Powell spoke of people who mentored him, helping him to see the value in encouraging others, giving them room to grow, and encouraging them to develop their ideas, try them out, and learn from mistakes when they hit bumps.

Powell's own experiences reflect a cultural thread expressed by many people—General Mills values the person and will work with you to ensure that you find your place. People may be in their sweet spot with the very first job that they get at General Mills, or it may take more time and a few different moves—yet when people are genuinely invited in, and asked to share and then implement some of their ideas, the investment that they have in their career and the success of the company is heightened tremendously. What is distinctive about this approach at General Mills is that the emphasis is placed on genuinely listening to people's ideas first and then determining how and where they might fit in.

When a leader makes a habit of seeking ideas, she may routinely hear great thoughts about how to improve a function in the tech department from someone working in HR. If that person in HR ever signals restlessness or discontent with the HR position, the leader already knows to steer him toward a role in the tech department. Yet in a company where seeking ideas is not part of the culture, leaders and managers might never see the strength or skill set in that employee— and would risk losing him to another company.

One manager spoke of the ways in which he is able to help support members of his sales team to pursue their own success. Mainly, he said, he works to make sure those who report to him are not seen as competitors. "Instead, we're encouraged to create an environment where I can say as a manager 'I don't want to see you succeed as much as me, but even more than me.' I think people are encouraged by that and will work even harder for you."

Significantly, this practice of encouraging people to excel and try out new ideas isn't reserved for just salaried workers; the culture is experienced by hourly employees as well. An hourly production worker said, "Everyone who works here has the opportunity to be a part of things that affect their job. You can be part of a special project, be on one of the many committees, or submit a suggestion. Participants in these programs will get their ideas and thoughts heard about things that affect their working life."

General Mills has a very diverse population of employees—diverse on a number of the traditional diversity measures, but also in terms of the types of positions people hold and the international nature of the company. In fact, Powell's own experiences working abroad for General Mills taught him about the importance of seeking diverse points of view and the value of an active stance on inclusion that seeks to bring in ideas from all the different sources in an organization.

After about ten years at General Mills headquarters, Powell was offered a position in a joint venture between General Mills and Nestlé that required him to move to the UK. "I was in the UK five years and Switzerland for seven," he said—first as the head of marketing and then as the CEO of the joint venture. "It was a great opportunity—the company was really lean, and we needed everyone. We had seventy-five people in the head office but it was a very global company, competing in a hundred and thirty countries around the world. We built fifteen to sixteen plants all over the world and created marketing approaches for all of this. I did that for eleven years and lived in an airplane, traveled around the world, worked with people from everywhere. When we talk about multicultural and inclusion and you work in that environment, there's only one way to do it. You just include everybody; you have to, it's very clear. Of seventy-five people in the office, we had twenty-three different nationalities. It was fun, it was really a lot of fun.

"I learned that you have to appreciate the team and the talent you have around you and figure out how you'll contribute as a leader," he continued, "and it certainly wouldn't be by trying to tell the manager in France what to do with her sales force. I think it works best to develop a much more collegial approach to things with much more debate. At the end, my job was to crystallize things into core strategies that would be fundamental and drive the organization forward. It became very much an appreciation of the expertise around me. Some people struggle with this. No one has all the answers, and this was a case where that was abundantly clear—and for me, working with this great team and getting to hear their ideas and work with that was challenging and fun."

Powell had some signature experiences during this time that he has carried with him into his current role as CEO. He has taken a stance on inclusion based on his own work with people around the world, seeing everyone as valuable and setting them up to share their ideas and collaborate for the long-term success of the business. Powell's opportunities came to him through work assignments; you may need to more actively seek out opportunities to work with people who are different from you. Asking for those experiences or creating them yourself could lead to a great deal of enjoyment as you learn to see things from different perspectives and benefit from new ideas. It's highly likely that your work projects will be more successful as well.

> When I was being recruited I was brought here to meet people, see Minneapolis and General Mills. One of my questions was what would it be like to be a single black woman in Minneapolis. It was nothing to do with General Mills, but that was a key aspect of my decision to come here. They set up a weekend visit so I could get a sense of the city and recommended some churches for me, that I'd asked about. I also met with Mark Addicks, our chief marketing officer. The fact that they would have him meet with me to help me in my decision making was amazing. He told me, "We want this to be a good decision for you. Our goal is to answer your questions at the end of the day, no matter what you decide." There was no pressure; it was just about making sure I made the right decision.
>
> —*General Mills employee*

SHARING THE BENEFITS

After people have joined an organization, there is often a honeymoon period when the glow of the new job, resources, and relationships is expressed through a person's commitment and hard work. Yet that glow can wear off after a year or so if the reality is different from what was promised.

One of the distinctions of a Trustworthy Leader—a distinction that carries through to the great companies in which they work—is an ability to ensure that the glow that most employees experience during their first years carries forward throughout their careers. An important way to do this is to reinforce a person's sense of his or her personal value to the organization. This occurs in part through an emphasis on growth throughout a career, which will be covered in more detail in Chapter Six. But an employee's value is also reinforced through sharing the benefits that are created by the organization; this comes from the influence of a trusted leader—and that leader's stance on inclusion.

A leader's success in the area of inclusion, as with all of the elements in the Virtuous Circle, is dependent in part on the consistency of actions and words. Were the promises made during the recruiting process kept? Was the culture represented true to a culture that still exists? Trustworthy Leaders are able to make good on the recruitment and welcoming sheen: they find ways to equitably reward people throughout their careers, to fully include them in the company and in its successes. This confirms to people that they are seen as valuable to the organization beyond the initial recruiting and hiring period.

At ACIPCO (American Cast Iron Pipe Company), based in Birmingham, Alabama, the practice of inclusion began over a hundred years ago, before anyone had ever applied the word to the actions of leaders in business. John Eagan, the first president of ACIPCO and one of its original investors, was a Southern pioneer for racial justice, civic reform, and labor relations, and he nurtured ACIPCO into a thriving company built on a foundation of theocracy. His philosophy materialized in the form of employee benefits unheard of in the early twentieth century: ACIPCO employees had a voice in company matters through profit sharing, an employee suggestion system, and on-site medical services. This was all decades before these programs found their way into other manufacturing companies, or into any industry, really.

So dedicated was Eagan to his workforce, and so confident in their ability to be good stewards of company resources, that before his death in 1924 he placed the common stock of ACIPCO into a trust with employees as beneficiaries. This singular act from Eagan's vision for the company transferred ownership and cemented in place the foundation that still guides the company's operations.

Employees continue to receive many benefits and services as a result of the Eagan Trust. These include medical and dental services, a noncontributory pension plan, and a number of other fringe benefits. A profit-sharing bonus plan permits employees to share any profits that may be earned. And the result of all of this? ACIPCO has a reputation for regularity of work and good employee relations, along with an astonishingly low turnover rate of between 1 and 2 percent. One of the oldest employee suggestion systems in the country encourages employee participation in improving practices in all areas of the business. Van Richey has been ACIPCO's CEO for the past twenty years, and he has continued in the tradition of Eagan to do what he knows to be right, ensuring that ACIPCO operates from a stance of inclusion.

Another company that takes a fierce stance on letting people know that they are valued is Robert W. Baird & Co. Baird is an investment and financial services company with about 2,600 employees, based in Milwaukee, Wisconsin. Baird traces its roots back to the creation of First Wisconsin Company, the securities arm of First Wisconsin National Bank. It was not until 1948 that the company's name was changed to Robert W. Baird & Co., after its former president. Although the Baird name did not represent the company until nearly thirty years after its founding, the influence of Baird's leadership on the company's culture began immediately with Robert Baird's expressed commitment to honesty and integrity in all services and a focus on meeting client needs. This influence of leader values on the culture at Baird has continued through successive leadership changes, up to and including the influence of the current president, Paul Purcell.

Purcell is a very energetic person, given to enthusiastic greetings, strong points of view that are clearly expressed, and a dynamic leadership style that he characterizes as one of urgency. When he took the helm, his plans for Baird's growth were more aggressive than those of his predecessor, Fred Kasten, who had been Baird's president for twenty-one years. Although their leadership goals were very different, their leadership *values* were virtually identical. "What we wanted for the firm was similar, but how we would get there was different. I am a very urgent person. He was not as urgent. I would break more china than he would, and I was a better change agent. What brought me here was our similar values about integrity, taking care of the client, and the dignity of everybody who works here. In financial services, the dignity of the individual is really hard to find."

When he first took over, Purcell wanted to ensure that all of the practices at Baird were pointing in the same direction—one that included everyone in the values of the firm and that equitably shared the value created. This meant that training and development opportunities needed to be offered to everyone, the ability to live a balanced life needed to be available to all, and everyone should share in the financial rewards of the workplace. It is in this last stance—on the equitable distribution of the financial rewards produced by the company—that Baird has taken an approach unique to its industry—actually, unique among many industries. With its equitable distribution of rewards, Purcell and other firm leaders have affirmed the singular role that leaders need to play in living out their belief that every individual deserves to be included and treated with dignity.

Purcell's first year as CEO was an active one, and he has continued in that vein. "It was very important emotionally, psychologically, and financially that we be in control of our destiny as a company," Purcell said. "This was part of the plan from day one, because we have really talented people, and what really talented people want is to run their business. We do plans, we sit down and ask if people have the resources to run their businesses. We ask if they understand what is expected of them, and we check in with them in six to twelve months. That's what really good people want. That's what adults want. We're a really flat organization, and we get people who are adults and teamwork-oriented.

"Every single employee gets a bonus tied to profits," he continued. "This includes our hourly associates and last year their bonus was 9.5 percent of base. Everybody participates in the profits. Second, we take approximately 10–12 percent of pre-tax profits and we put it into profit-sharing. That's a really big number, and it's in addition to a 401(k) match of up to $2,000 per person. Approximately half of our employees are shareholders. Over half our people get paid three different ways in addition to their base compensation, and they share in what we do. Everyone feels important and part of the place."

Purcell is an avid capitalist, and he does not shrink from criticizing his industry for practices that he believes do not reward what he finds to be the honor and integrity of capitalism. "Maybe meritocracy is a better word. We're an investment banking firm, so it can't be socialism. Everybody is not equal, and they don't get paid the same, but everybody gets treated well, so that they absolutely believe that what they do is important—because it is. The mail guy is important. He's part of the game."

Purcell believes inclusion on this scale not only is an ethical way to treat people, but reaps business benefits as well. "I think, unfortunately, our industry for the most part is all about money and greed. New York believes everything is about power and money; but not everything is about power and money. At 2 A.M., when that analyst sees that a number is wrong, he has the choice to stay til 4 A.M. and fix it, or go home. That's not about power and money, and he's so tired that it's not about fear either. He either says, 'I am a professional and I am going to get this right,' or he doesn't care. That choice comes from a belief system. You want the mail guy to be really good, and you want the receptionist to be the best receptionist. You want everybody, no matter what their job is, to take pride in their job and believe that it makes a difference. If they do, then that bottom up lives on its own oxygen. You have to have a soul to do that. You have to believe that it's really important. You have to believe it's the right thing to do from a human point of view, and you have to know that it's the right thing to do from a corporate strategy point of view. We are privately held and employee owned because for us that is the best approach for executing this strategy."

These are forceful words from a very dynamic leader, words that convey the strength and depth of his conviction that every single person who works at Baird is important. This strength of conviction is found throughout the Trustworthy Leaders at Baird and among the employees as well. Although the words used may not be quite as assertive, the meaning is the same.

Baird's stance on the equitable treatment of all has translated into some key elements of success in the marketplace. Senior leaders at Baird are unequivocal in their linking of the company culture to their financial success, regularly affirming that in fact it is *the major differentiator* between Baird and its competitors. The challenging economic climate has only emphasized that differentiation.

Since the beginning of 2007, Baird successfully recruited more than 175 experienced professionals to positions at the officer level of senior vice president or above across many of its business units. Many of these highly regarded veterans could have chosen to work at top Wall Street firms, often for more money than they would receive at Baird. Yet they chose Baird, and they often cited the strong culture as the reason why. In 2010 Baird's voluntary turnover rate was 7.3 percent compared to the 19-percent national average for private sector companies in the United States. Baird is a very successful orga-

> When I transitioned to Baird, I was shocked and surprised at how everybody was so willing to work together for the common good, which was most importantly your client. It was looking for ways to say yes before we have to say no. Everybody pulls together, and it is incredibly refreshing. I, too, look at it as a blessing every day.
>
> —*Baird employee*

The people here really respect you for what you do. They are easy to talk to. It's easy to work here and get my job done. In doing that, I can sleep well and come into work and talk to people without feeling like they were being condescending or that there were ulterior motives. I didn't realize how difficult it was, how political and territorial, and how much people hoarded information when I was at another place. I guess when you're in a place like that you just think that's how work is. A lot of my friends can't believe it when I tell them what it's like here.

—*Baird employee*

nization in terms of their culture, their reputation in the community, and their financial performance. People understand why and work very hard to protect and promote the integrity of everything that they do.

CONTINUING THE CIRCLE

When a leader acts from a sense of honor, you will also see an inclusive work environment. Leaders who express humility, encourage reciprocity, and show awareness of their position will be sure to clear the front steps so that people who are invited into the organization see a path that is open.

Just as important, if you notice a work environment that is inclusive—in which people are free to be themselves, are connecting with one another regardless of background or title, and share equitably in the benefits—you should take a close look at that company's leader. You will likely see all the earmarks of someone operating from a sense of honor. The two qualities are complementary and intertwined.

Both honor and inclusion represent a philosophical stance. Though they certainly manifest in a leader's actions, at their foundation they are conceptual. They are about how a leader feels and how a leader thinks, and they are grounded in a leader's inherent values and the scores of experiences that shape a leader throughout his or her life. Honor and inclusion underlie not only how a leader leads, but who a leader is.

How do you tap into this, to your own inherent values and experiences? Some people believe that values are unchangeable, that you come with what you grew up with. And while early influences are significant, your experiences can help you to uncover deeply held values that perhaps you haven't yet fully expressed. Experiences can be examined and learned from years after they happened, and certainly new experiences can be pursued. Just as thinking about honor is important, so is reviewing experiences, looking for lessons, and pursuing new experiences that might bring you into contact with people who are different from you—on whatever criteria you choose.

As you develop your leadership approach, ask people who have had different experiences than you to describe their approach, their strategies. Ask them to tell you, as best they can, what they think happened that got them to hold the values they do and then ask them whether they are able to put their values into practice. Then ask yourself the same questions.

The more aware we are as human beings about what drives our behavior and our choices to do one thing over another, the more opportunity we create for ourselves to make a shift, to act with greater clarity with respect to our values. If you want to be a Trustworthy Leader, then understanding what drives your behavior towards others and your ability to be inclusive will be critical to your success.

In the next three chapters—Valuing Followership, Sharing Information, and Developing Others—we move from the realm of values and philosophy into the work being carried out on the ground. Yet this stance that has been developed by Trustworthy Leaders of honor and inclusion will be visible in all of the "on the ground" actions that leaders take and support in others. It is all part of the Virtuous Circle that Trustworthy Leaders develop and lead from as they move through their careers.

Uncovering the Roots of Inclusion

How does a senior leader come to develop a stance on inclusion that supports a genuine interest in others, a willingness to listen to their ideas, and a commitment to the equitable sharing of benefits when so much of our current corporate structure pretends to value the exact opposite? Bob Giles, managing partner of Perkins Coie, is someone who would be seen as a "typical" successful lawyer on paper. He is white, male, over fifty, and financially successful. Yet he is unique in his outspoken commitment to inclusion and in his willingness to take action. Giles attributes his commitment to inclusion to an experience he had early in his career.

Giles explained, "Very early on as a managing partner, I went to one of these Myers-Briggs training sessions—and really was convinced by that experience that a diverse group of people can consider more information and make better decisions." The trainer brought two groups of people up to the front of the room. One group was identified as "Sensers" and the other was identified as "Intuiters," according to the Myers-Briggs inventory. The trainer told the audience that he would show each group an object, and they would then be asked to write about it as a group. He showed both groups an apple and then sent them off to private rooms to write about it. After the two groups had left the training session, he told the rest of the participants that in about thirty seconds, he predicted that someone from the "Sensers" group would ask, on behalf of the group, to have the apple. Sure enough, someone stuck her head into the room and asked for the apple.

The trainer then proceeded to tell the audience what he believed would be the tone of the two descriptions that would come back from these different groups of people. Again, his prediction was spot-on. The Sensers gave a very concise description of the apple—its size, coloring, and other specific characteristics. The Intuiters described "amber waves of grain and health and the growth of the apple on the tree."

Giles was both stunned and fascinated that two groups of comparably skilled, comparably trained, and equally intelligent people could approach the same situation with such predictably distinct perspectives. "I really developed an appreciation for the different ways that people approach things," he said of the experience.

Another example that was presented at this session also had a very clear impact on Giles's understanding of the power of different viewpoints within an organization. In this example, the same situation was considered by two different "boards of directors." Each board was composed of members with different ways of feeling and thinking. Giles said that "you could really see how the composition of the board affected what they considered and the perspective of the decision that they made. I was struck by some of the things that one group considered—when you heard about it after the fact, you'd say well sure, that should have been a part of the decision—but the other group just didn't think about it—I didn't think about it. So very early on, I became an advocate of not having 'yes' people, but of bringing in people with different perspectives, because it would help me to make the best decisions, help the executive committee to make the best decisions."

Giles did not change his own perspective so much as he realized the importance of opening up his mind to the thought processes of others. Doing so would give him the best information he could use to make decisions. And, he figured, if it would be of benefit to him in his work to receive information from a broad group of people and a variety of perspectives, then surely it would help the firm and their clients as well. "I often look at data and make an evaluation. If someone wants to talk to me about a problem, I want to solve the problem. So here were these examples of ways in which I could do a better job of solving problems based on who was a member of the group discussing the problems. When I saw this benefit of having multiple viewpoints come to life in these training sessions, it made sense. So I've just gone with that approach ever since."

Importantly, Giles is able to convey his perspective to everyone he consults with at work, ensuring that people understand his belief in their value to the organization. "Because they know that I don't bring people in as tokens," he said, "that I will listen to them, they join up. We've had some pretty significant discussions, and I don't mind that—but when we finally make a decision, we have to go forward together. Even if I haven't changed my mind, I may have changed my perspective."

CHAPTER FOUR

VALUING FOLLOWERSHIP

Imagine you are watching an orchestra perform. What do you see? A conductor, waving his baton this way and the other, encouraging the strings to come in at just the right time, the winds at another, and finally, at just the right moment, the percussion. The conductor will be the first individual who takes a bow at the end—after all, he's been on the podium, in the "leadership" position, creating the beautiful music you've enjoyed all evening. But what would he be accomplishing without musicians willing to follow his lead? There would be no music— just an odd person in a tuxedo waving a wand, and lots of noise emanating from individual instruments, sometimes in sync, yet at others, clashing.

A great conductor understands that in order to be effective, it's all about those musicians and whether they're willing to follow him. Without followers, he is standing alone either in silence or in discordant chaos. A Trustworthy Leader understands this as well—that leadership success is inextricably linked to people's willingness to follow.

Although the topic of followership does get stirred up at times in the leadership literature, mostly it remains below the surface of the big flash of new ideas and theories about how to be a "better" leader. In most reports the leader is still at the center of it all, the one who makes the difference. It is his or her efforts that are singularly praised and analyzed. Yet this is not the case in great workplaces.

During my interviews with senior leaders at Best Companies, I always heard comments and stories about the importance of followers. Leaders talked about engaging followers when they spoke of their own work, what they enjoyed most, the lessons learned, and their plans for the future. Yet in our current public consciousness, I've yet to see widespread recognition that the great leaders are those who are most respectful of their followers.

During much of my formative study about life in organizations—first as a graduate student, then as a professor, and during my initial consulting days—the stories to read were often about leaders like "Chainsaw" Al Dunlap of Scott Paper and Sunbeam-Oster, whose claim to fame was his decisiveness and willingness to cut people out of the organization without a second thought. Or there were stories about GE's Jack Welch, whose infamous forced ranking system was used to do the same thing, but with a professional flair that received more positive acclaim. The focus for both of these leaders was on their ability to rank and separate, to promote some and get rid of others, so that the organization could make money—as much as possible. The consequences of these actions for the followers were sometimes discussed—the layoffs, hardships, impact on the community—but they were accepted as the consequences of smart business practices and strong leadership.

At that time there was a small group of people who pointed out that these practices were harmful and destructive of both present and future value within the organization, yet their collective voice remained under the louder, sometimes screaming voices of people wanting to celebrate the actions of great, tough leaders taking aggressive action to lead the way—pulling people with them or throwing them overboard if they had to.

In 1994, Warren Bennis was one voice of reason trying to change the discussion about leaders and followers. A notable chronicler of leadership behavior himself, he explained our fascination with people such as Chainsaw Al and Jack Welch as inevitable, given our starstruck culture. Yet he also saw it as misplaced:

> As a long-time student and teacher of management, I, too, have tended to look to the men and women at the top for clues on how organizations achieve and maintain institutional health. But the longer I study effective leaders, the more I am convinced of the underappreciated importance of effective followers. . . . In a world of growing complexity, leaders are increasingly dependent on their subordinates for good information, whether the leaders want to hear it or not. Followers who tell the truth, and leaders who listen to it, are an unbeatable combination.[1]

Bennis's ideas on the importance of followership did not spread widely at the time, yet they have contributed to a recent shift in attention to the interplay of leadership and followership. Professors and social psychologists Stephen Reicher, Alexander Haslam, and Michael Platow have argued that the key to leadership is found beyond the person *as an individual* and instead resides in the leader's activities as a functioning *group member*. What many people have called leadership in the past, these authors cite as a simple exercise of power: "When leaders resort to brute force, it needs to be understood that essentially they are using power, not leading. This is the distinction between 'power over' and 'power through.' The latter is identity-based; the former is resource-based and is not true leadership."[2]

Which brings us back to Al Dunlap and Jack Welch, whose exercise of power was often presented as leadership. Welch's approach was generally considered to be kinder than Dunlap's, yet both of them fell on the same side of the leadership spectrum, choosing to use "power over" rather than "power through." Although both men were able to accomplish many things, think of what more they could have accomplished if their actions had been based in a respectful appreciation of *all* of their followers. People would have still been fired at times, and there would always be stronger performers and weaker performers, yet with respectful appreciation, the distractions of brute force would have been minimized, and the potential for collective success maximized.

There is much about valuing followership that takes root in the honor and inclusion beliefs of Trustworthy Leaders. Honor and inclusion provide the philosophical underpinnings, the background, for the actions it takes to engage followers. To go back to our orchestra metaphor, think of honor and inclusion as the knowledge and sensibility that great conductors everywhere bring into the concert hall with them. They are well prepared to deliver a quality performance before they've taken up their batons and the first note has been played.

The leaders from the three companies I discuss in the rest of this chapter are very different from leaders like Dunlap and Welch. These Trustworthy Leaders and their followers create situations in which the interplay between leading and following does away with the stereotype of the all-knowing or command-and-control leader. Leaders can be kind, ask questions, admit doubt during the decision-making process, and enjoy the discussion and camaraderie of followers. They also can and do present their positions strongly and clearly. Followers as well avoid stereotypes: they are not "yes" people; they are "I can do this" people. They are able to be themselves with no diminishment of their smarts, ideas, or dreams. They are participants in the work of the organization, able to contribute with dignity—whatever the specific task is that they are engaged in. The ability to follow with dignity contributes to the new dynamic: both leader and follower are necessary for the work of the organization to get done, and both are able to make their contributions with their personal identity and integrity intact.

So what do Trustworthy Leaders do to engage followers? How do they cultivate the practice of followership within their organizations? For one, Trustworthy Leaders recognize that following is a *choice*—a point of tremendous significance that contrasts with compliance-based behavior that I call *pseudo-followership*. Following based in compliance occurs when people are apathetic, are working from a place of singular self-interest, or are working in an environment of fear. When fear enters the relationship, honest feedback to the leader is lost, along with opportunities for creative idea sharing and inspired contributions. Trustworthy Leaders do all they can to ensure that people in their organizations *choose* to follow based on a shared identity and commitment, rather than following based on compliance.

Once a person has made the choice to follow, Trustworthy Leaders continue to build a relationship by making it clear that they want an active participant to *accompany* them—on the project, into the future, or in a specific new venture. When people accompany each other, they are informed of the direction in which they are headed, they are given the tools to contribute, and they are asked to speak up—to tell the truth.

Finally, Trustworthy Leaders seek out ways to *connect* with people to inspire followership. They wish to know and be known so they can develop strong bonds with people, bonds that will deepen as the entire group moves forward.

These three elements—choice, accompaniment, and connection—guide a Trustworthy Leader's approach to followership.

CHOICE

The role of choice in the leader-follower relationship is complex and has three distinct threads to it. The first is the most immediately apparent one: when followers choose their leader, the connection between them is stronger and the communication is more open. When people choose to follow, it is a sign of their respect for the leader and an acknowledgment of the confidence they have in the leader's integrity.

In order for people to follow you by choice, you need to create the conditions that convey your trustworthiness and invite people into the organization in such a way that it's clear they do indeed have a choice. If you fail to do this, then you will get compliance behavior, which gets employees to do the task required, but nothing more. The employee's personal needs—for job security, income, or a stepping stone to the next position—will end up being the most important ones that guide her decisions.

The choice of a leader very rarely stops there, which introduces the second thread: when people are empowered to choose their leader, more than likely they are also empowered to choose in other areas of their work. This creates more ownership in that work, more pride and investment, and ultimately a better final product.

And third, when choice is a factor in the leader-follower relationship, it is rarely just about the CEO as leader and everyone else as follower. Rather, the spirit of it runs throughout the organization as a whole, such that followers seamlessly become leaders at times, and vice versa, leading to an environment in which the best person for the job at hand is empowered to step up and is given the support of her team. Richer, fuller music results as the orchestra expands.

Of all the companies that I have studied over the past many years, the one that rises to the top when it comes to clearly articulating the interplay of leadership and followership, and that provides an excellent example of the role of choice in the process, is W. L. Gore & Associates. Gore was founded in 1958 by Bill and Vieve Gore, in the basement of their home, to serve the electronic products market. While the company has been known for the unique success, creativity, and innovativeness of their products, it is also known as an organization in which cultural creativity, integrity, and respect thrive.

Much of the literature about economic downturns warns leaders that "Your best people will leave when the market gets tough." They will be the most sought after by others and thus have the most freedom to move elsewhere when things turn sour. This has happened at many companies in which the connection between employee and leader is based primarily on the employment contract as opposed to resting on a strong, trust-based leader-follower relationship. When followership is strong, the best people do not leave. They haven't left at Gore, where voluntary turnover was near 3 percent in 2010, or less than half of the Best Companies average that year (which is itself less than half of the national average given by the Bureau of Labor Statistics). When people have chosen to follow leaders they trust, they will stick with them through thick and thin. One longtime Gore employee has heard associates who have been at Gore as little as a year saying of their leaders, "I would follow them anywhere."

What happens at Gore is special. For one, people do not have titles; instead, everyone is known as an associate. Associates are actively involved in choosing what projects they want to work on. They are also involved in choosing their leaders. At Gore, a leader is defined as an associate who has followers. If no one wants to follow you, you won't become a leader. Gore's workplace, when described by outsiders, is often talked about as an anomaly, possibly because the sense of equality and lack of hierarchy throw people off. We have an expectation that people will have titles and positions that convey power, influence, and status, yet at Gore that's not the case.

People at Gore have influence because of their competence and skill, and they have status because they are all valued human beings who work in an organization whose culture rests on the belief that each person is worthy of respect. The word *power* is not used often there, except when people talk about the power of a certain piece of machinery. And so it can be difficult for outsiders to wrap their minds around a place that works so well—with its own ups and downs, yet without many of the traditional trappings of organization structure. While what happens at W. L. Gore & Associates is distinctive, it is also instructive. From their example, we can understand what happens when leading and following work well together in the practice of Trustworthy Leadership.

Terri Kelly, the current CEO and one of the few people who actually has a specific title at Gore (to fulfill legal requirements), gave some insight into the strength of Gore's culture and the role of followership in the company's tremendous success. At Gore, people are invited into the organization and asked to be themselves. Current associates look for new team members who have skills and abilities that will be of benefit to the organization. Yet they also look for an independence of mind and a willingness to commit to the culture of the organization.

People who join Gore will go through many interviews before they are offered a position. The job offer is actually an invitation: to join the organization within a certain core commitment area, explore, and then make further commitments to contribute in specific ways. As new associates gain a greater understanding of their work and the business, they have the latitude to shape and expand beyond their initial core commitment. Your commitments end up being your work responsibilities—what other people would call a job description. People are given training, support, and time—and they are asked, as a part of their commitment to the organization, to commit to follow someone. At Gore, every step in the leader-follower dynamic is a choice.

Kelly herself became the CEO through this same dynamic. She joined Gore in 1983 as a process engineer, and over the past decades many people have chosen to follow her lead.

In 2004, when Gore's then-CEO indicated that he was ready to step away from that commitment, the company started looking for a new leader. Associates at Gore are regularly reviewed by their peers and their team, and the search for a CEO was no different. The company's peer-based leadership selection process kicked into gear, and Kelly emerged as the next CEO, not because she lobbied for the position, but because her peers lobbied for her; they wanted to follow her lead.

Kelly spends a lot of time talking with associates. She has noticed that newer associates are much more inquisitive about the beliefs and values as well as the financial strength of the organization—more so than when she started at the company twenty-six years ago. "It's not just about 'what's the job?' and 'what can I expect to be doing?'" she said of questions she gets from them. "It's more trying to get at the foundation of what the company is all about . . . they are much more aware of how quickly that can shift or how vulnerable joining even large multinational companies can be if you don't really understand the underlying health of the company."

These new associates are starting to define why they would actively choose to follow someone at Gore. When an associate begins work, he or she is encouraged to spend considerable time understanding the culture and building relationships—talking with people, learning how things get done, and building a network. While there are sponsors and coaches who provide guidance to new associates, to help them navigate Gore's cultural practices, there is much observing, participating, and asking of questions that needs to happen for new associates to really become a member of the organization. This emphasis on learning rather than making an immediate impact can be a bit unnerving for a new associate, anxious to contribute, yet it reinforces the importance of not just what you accomplish, but how you accomplish it.

As Kelly explained, understanding the culture takes time. And Gore gives people that time. "We're really cautious to say, 'Take your time,' you know, six months or a year. It's very frustrating at the early stage because people don't feel they're earning their worth. What they don't recognize is that this is that rare opportunity to soak it all in, learn before they make a big decision or a big mistake. You're really trying to understand how things work, and the only way you can learn that is to be immersed in that environment and have folks help you learn how to best do this in the context of the Gore culture." Because Gore is so attentive to the time and attention it takes to help associates make those first connections and choices, they have to invest in personnel slowly and carefully. They have to make sure each new employee has coaching and mentorship, so they don't try to assimilate too many people at once.

Interestingly, what happens when you are empowered to choose your work, and to choose a leader in this way, is that the leader-follower relationship becomes more fluid. One person might lead a project but then slip into the role of follower when that makes sense, only to take the leader reins once more when the situation is appropriate. Letting people choose to follow also supports their ability to choose to lead. This creates an amazing system in which leadership and followership dance together in partnership, creating a powerful experience for everyone.

One associate provided some examples of this dance as he spoke of the opportunities for people to choose to be leaders and followers. "To be a successful leader at Gore," he said, "you have to have developed followership. It was very interesting when I started to see how this is not just a concept, it truly is how leadership works here. If you're in a leadership position and you don't have followership, you're not going to stay in that position. You won't be successful as a leader. To develop followership, you use more influence-type skills than you do management skills."

The associate finds the leader-follower relationship incredibly rewarding, because as you're developing your followers, you're also developing them to become leaders. "It's very much a circle, where sometimes you step forward and take the lead on an issue, but then, as a leader, you can look at your team and say, 'Who can step forward this time and take the lead on this?' In some ways, it takes some of the pressure off because you're looking at your whole team as an ensemble and saying, 'Who can benefit from stepping forward on this issue?'" In this way, leaders face less stress in their roles as leaders when they are able to share leadership opportunities, and they can actually choose to be a follower for a while, letting someone else lead. It is no diminishment of their role or importance in the organization—especially in a place like Gore—as everyone knows that they are valuable.

Another associate and leader remarked, "I see leadership potential in lots of people, and it's all situational, based on what's required, and people do that all day long here in all walks of life, no matter what kind of function you're in."

So, can people be great followers if their leaders are not great? At Gore the answer is no; thus they seek to ensure that they have great leaders so that others can focus on following. Following is not the sum total of someone's work—it has to do with the way that people interact and make decisions, and it is a choice. Following is not less than leading, it is simply different. People at Gore see one another's abilities as valuable and acknowledge that different people need to do different things at different times: some want to and are able to lead; others want to and are able to follow; and this can switch depending on the circumstances. Associates at Gore need to be good at what they do (their technical expertise), but they also need to be good leaders and followers.

Aspiring Trustworthy Leaders would do well to take a few lessons from Gore. Leaders are best able to fulfill their responsibilities when the people who work with them have chosen to follow them. This creates a dynamic of active participation as opposed to simple compliance. Leadership is less stressful when leadership opportunities are shared. And leading with followers who choose creates a situation in which the leader is actively supported by people—and challenged and questioned as well, yet it is all done in a system of support.

As Gore proves, there are excellent reasons a Trustworthy Leader should create a relationship of choice for followers. Perhaps it won't be as culturally ingrained as it is at Gore, yet there are definite steps a leader can take to increase the likelihood that followers have a choice in the matter. Simple things like asking people who follow you for their input prior to making a decision can increase a person's sense that their contributions have value. Letting people make the choices that they are best equipped to make can increase their sense that they are being respected—and perhaps offer them a chance at leadership if they are also able to implement the choice they've made.

> What's helped me be successful is knowing when to lead and knowing when to follow. I think there's this misperception at times that as leaders we need to have it all figured out, when in reality, I've got to hand off the ball when the knowledge expert is someone other than myself. The leadership aspect is very situational. It's when it's time to lead and when it's time to follow, and really successful leaders at Gore do that very well. They're willing to be vulnerable and hand that ball off and not feel any remorse or disappointment in that.
>
> —Gore associate

If you are the designated leader of a group yet are able to step back at times and follow someone else's lead— and explain your reasons why—then that can help to shift the dynamic of a permanent one-way leader-follower exchange to one in which leaders and followers can share their responsibilities. It may also be that in talking with people who follow you, it becomes clear that some of them would rather be doing something else. Perhaps there is another leader they would rather follow or another position or area of the company they'd rather work in. If you are successful in helping those people to find their sweet spot, then your own leadership credentials will be enhanced, making it more likely that the people who do follow you will feel positive about their own choices. It's all part of the relationships that people form and the mutual respect that develops when you are able to choose who you want to follow.

ACCOMPANIMENT

In a musical presentation, accompaniment is the action of playing along with other musicians as a supporter of their performance. The work of an accompanist is intended to add to the entire presentation, to bring it to completion. It is intended to complement what is already there, providing symmetry and balance to the other parts that make up the entire composition. With an orchestra, ensemble, or other musical performance that isn't a solo act, the beauty comes from the balance created from everyone's contributions. The idea of the performance already exists—the musical score—yet the reality of the perform-ance happens only when people start contributing, playing off of each other's contributions, creating more from what occurs together than each individual person's contribution.

If we think of the work activities that occur in a great organization and the creativity and innovation that are tapped into through collaborative work, the notion of people accompanying each other is an appropriate and powerful metaphor. And as with most every-thing in a great workplace, it starts with the actions of Trustworthy Leaders who create the culture and the environment in which this can happen.

In many great organizations, people talk about the extraordinary sense of the place: that it feels different, that there is a sense of electricity to people's movements and in the overall atmosphere. This happens when Trustworthy Leaders create the conditions through which followers are invited to accompany them on the journey. Followers' contributions are acknowledged as powerful, necessary, and valued elements that create the overall music of the workplace.

Practicing the art of accompaniment is one of the ways in which an idea like reciprocity, discussed in Chapter Two, can be built on and expanded. Reciprocity starts with a belief in the value of others' contributions, and when the practice of seeking those ideas becomes continuous, it contributes to the creativity and forward movement that are at the heart of accompaniment. The music created by a leader and followers as they accompany each other is part of what followers describe when they speak glowingly of their leaders and what outsiders feel when they walk into a great workplace.

Trustworthy Leaders are excellent at inviting followers into the work activities of the organization. They take specific and unique steps, both immediate and long term, to create and sustain the sense of accompaniment that will make their organization special. An excellent example of an organization in which the practice of accompaniment is in full operation is CH2M HILL, an engineering and construction firm that has been recognized over the years as one of the Best Companies in the United States and in Australia, one of the Most Admired Companies in the United States, and as one of the World's Most Ethical Companies.

CH2M HILL is an employee-owned company, with twenty-three thousand employees around the world. Their growth has been both internal and through acquisitions. The founders started the CH2M part of the company in 1946, adding the "HILL" part through a merger in 1971. All of them agreed that respect, delivery excellence, and employee control would be the central values. Bob Allen, the former senior vice president of Human Resources, describes the organization's durability as grounded in these roots. "I don't think sixty years ago, folks sat down and said, 'This is the kind of company we want to be when we are $6–7 billion.' It started out with the four founders deciding that they liked to work with each other. They set out some values for themselves, and those values still exist today. That's the core essence of the company." Following the values established by the founders has guided leaders at CH2M HILL as they have invited people into the organization, encouraged them to speak up, and integrated them into the collaborative culture.

One consistency that CH2M HILL has maintained over the years is a commitment to a flat organizational structure in which everyone knows that they are valuable, and all work together to "build a better world." In order for this to happen, people need to be able to talk with each other, collaborate, and trust that everyone's best interests are considered. As we saw with Gore, practices like this require time to be put into practice and utilized successfully.

Chairman and CEO Lee McIntire speaks to the empowerment that employees, on the whole, feel at the company when he says, "We're slower here to make decisions, and it's very consensus-oriented. I've learned you've got to take a little time. . . . Here it's very much directed from bottom up." Employees know that they make the decisions and they hold responsibility for their own success. Outsiders may raise questions, yet each project team is responsible for their own success. This sense of responsibility and ownership conveys the spirit of independence that pervades CH2M HILL, yet more importantly it conveys the sense of "us," which is a key ingredient in a Trustworthy Leader's approach to followership.

Allen said that employees have always been empowered to remind leaders of their core values every day. "Here," he said, "when people get off track—unlike a lot of companies where employees will complain about management in the lunchroom or at the bar—it is often in your face. It is an email that says, 'I don't like this' or it is an employee meeting and a leader gets called out. The environment allows folks to get comfortable calling out management about things they don't like or have problems with." Although this may sound more like confrontation than accompaniment, it is actually a very important part of the process of creating the trust that allows accompaniment to happen. People want to get it right. At CH2M HILL, the people at the job site are just as invested in the quality of the performance—in this case, the building projects—as are the leaders. So in order to get it right, to ensure high quality, people ask questions and test assumptions, so that when the project actually begins and people are at the building site laying the foundation, the entire group is in sync.

Great followers of Trustworthy Leaders are those who will speak up and know that their words will be heard, considered, and evaluated for their merit—not as a challenge to authority or questioning of the leader's right to be in that position. The Trustworthy Leaders at CH2M HILL may have their decisions challenged, yet the important role a follower plays in presenting that challenge will help the leader to better fulfill his responsibilities. This is beneficial followership, accompaniment at its best, and it's what Trustworthy Leaders in great workplaces are aiming for.

CH2M HILL's leaders—because of their heightened visibility to all—have had the weighty responsibility of continuously leading by example to remind others, and themselves, that the culture at CH2M HILL is what makes the place so special. "We are committed to a culture of Respect for People. This encompasses inclusion for all of our employees, acting with integrity, and valuing the diversity of our colleagues, clients, partners, and community members around the world," said John Madia, chief HR officer. "Our employees thrive here, and they feel comfortable sharing unique viewpoints and perspectives with colleagues at all levels of the organization." CH2M HILL's leaders strive to protect and encourage the culture wherever possible. To this end, special care is taken to hire and bring together a group of people who want to work with each other and with everyone else in the organization.

Bob Card, president of the Energy and Water Division, spoke of the time and energy spent on finding people who fit in well: "Whenever we recruited somebody, the first test was: Do they fit the firm? We didn't care how many degrees they had or what they had to offer. If they didn't fit personality-wise in the firm, we weren't interested. It's one of the things that I put on my list of reasons of why this is such a great company. We have, as a result, very few people who feel they need to leave here because they don't like the working environment. They get attracted occasionally somewhere else, but very few people pull the ripcord and say, 'I just can't deal with these people.'"

This emphasis on finding people who will fit in well, combined with the employee-controlled culture, has perpetuated an environment at CH2M HILL in which people are able to work alongside each other, with all contributing to the success of the project. Just as with a musical accompanist, the score (or project plan) is set and each person has his or her part that contributes to the overall quality and success of the experience.

A final way that leaders at CH2M HILL value followership and encourage accompaniment is found in the reasons why people are recognized and rewarded. People are recognized and rewarded for their talent, and an element of talent that is held in highest regard is an ability to collaborate and engage with people—accompanying them in their work.

Garry Higdem, president of the Transportation Business Group, shared that during a recent reorganization within the energy division, some people asked him for an organization chart. His response to them was, "It's not about the org chart. It's about the networking and the relationships—the collegial atmosphere of walking down the hall and seeing somebody and making the conversation happen. Keeping the dialogue moving."

Patrick O'Keefe, senior vice president of Corporate Affairs, said he feels that reward in the organization is based on relationship and value, that it's not either/or. "There's not value [if] you don't get along and there's not relationship without value. They'll reject you on both counts. There's much more use of 'we' than 'I' in conversation here. You have to get out of the first person. People who use 'I' too much don't last long. We've had some people who did not work out because they were too much about what they accomplished for everyone and not about what we accomplished together."

All this emphasis on collaboration and collegiality may appear too lofty or time-consuming to make good business sense, but not to CEO Lee McIntire, who is very clear on the powerful business benefits that come from these practices. When people accompany one another, when that electricity is palpable in a workplace, it translates to higher-quality work and a strong experience for the client. When people are accustomed to listening to their colleagues, of being respectful of their colleagues, then they are the same way with their customers. "Customers tell me that we're a little different than the competition," said McIntire. "I've had a number of these occasions where customers say that the reason they picked us is that we listen to the customers more. . . . We're up against the very best in the world, so we need some differentiator. A key client told me recently 'You listen better,' that that was why they chose our firm. I wrote that on my blog that night. It got tears in people's eyes."

At CH2M HILL, accompaniment works because everyone has a say in the business, leaders know the importance of respecting their followers, and people want to work with each other. The values of the organization are actually applied in day-to-day situations and are well integrated into the company's hiring and recognition practices. The quality of the firm's projects is well known in the marketplace and everyone inside the organization knows why. They are a talented group of people who have all chosen to be there, and everyone—leaders and followers—contributes to the success of what gets created.

The practice of accompaniment will look different in other organizations, yet the concept is certainly one that can be initiated by Trustworthy Leaders anywhere. It requires an ability and willingness on the part of leaders to see themselves as a distinct part of the process of the organization, yet not as the most important part of the process. Each person will have his or her place that is important

and distinct. A set of practices that follows from this simple acknowledgment includes emphasizing culture fit during hiring, encour-
aging open and honest conversations, and rewarding the talent you want in the organization. These acts reinforce what is special and unique in the culture and enable accompaniment to flourish. People will want to work in your organization and follow your lead.

> For me, it's like I'm running my own business. That's really important, because when you follow processes and you have a job description and you have a really set skill level and it's communicated well, they just let you go off and do it. They really treat you like adults. You are trusted to do exactly what you've agreed to do, and you deliver.
> —*CH2M HILL employee*

> The company believes that you're going to do a good job. You feel a huge sense of responsibility, and you want to deliver. At the same time, if you don't deliver you just hurt yourself.
> —*CH2M HILL employee*

CONNECTION

One of the experiences that people have when they work in a great organization is a strong and consistent sense that their leaders and managers are interested in them as people, not just as employees. The quality of this experience is a significant distinguishing characteristic that moves people's perception of their workplace from good to great. The personal relationship, the recognition that someone has a life outside of work that is important, and the ability to have a genuine conversation with people about the totality of their lives, are important ways in which Trustworthy Leaders create connections that bond them to their followers.

At a place like Gore, where leadership and followership are inter-changeable on a frequent basis, people's connections are obvious and deep. Stories abound of ways in which people know each other and how leaders and followers go out of their way to connect—asking about each other's families, travels, and hobbies as well as offering advice and support for challenges and triumphs. CH2M HILL also places an emphasis on connection, yet with a workforce of twenty-three thousand—many of them dispersed to job sites around the world—the ways in which people connect with each other are more varied and creative, as they often need to include consideration for time and distance. What's true everywhere, though, is the importance of creating connections and the responsibility of leaders to reach out to people, to take the initiative, as a sign of the value they place on their relationships with followers.

Another organization among the Best Companies in which connections between leaders and followers are deep, constant, and full of respect is Wegmans, a unique grocery store chain based in the northeastern United States. At Wegmans, followership is present, yet it is not spoken of with the same distinctness and detail as it is at Gore, nor with the same directness as at CH2M HILL. At Wegmans, followership and connection seem to occur as a natural extension of people growing up together, working together, and supporting each other. People who were once followers are now leaders, and they are extending to their new colleagues the same invitation to follow that they received when they first started.

The stories about connection at Wegmans are plentiful. Everyone I spoke with—whether it was Danny and Colleen Wegman, a store manager, or a stocker—had a story to tell about how they were cared for, listened to, or supported to learn and grow. And it always began with an invitation from a leader. Leaders' stories started with how they themselves were invited to form a connection when they first joined Wegmans, and how they pass it on. At Wegmans, creating connections is a way of life.

"We've all worked with one another at one point in our career," says an employee, "and you don't lose that relationship, you just continue the network. You've got people you can call who are experts, whether they are still working with you or at another store—you still have those relationships with them. You continue to build and develop them."

"'Comfort' is a word that comes to mind regardless of who I am interacting with or what their title or their stature is in the company," said another employee. "Bob Farr is the manager of one of the largest volume stores we have out there. Certainly a lot of respect goes to Bob and all the store managers out there, but I know as a person I can relate to Bob. I can relate to Kevin (vice president, store operations). They are out there building relationships. They are my leaders. I am a leader for a certain group of people, and we are trying to do the same thing with them. We're building that bond, so comfort is extremely important. We are not a company that's hung up on titles—who can I talk to, who can I not talk to. It's very people-oriented; you can make that quick connection."

For his part, Bob Farr says the same connection was offered to him when he began. "I remember coming here twenty-nine years ago," he said, "and walking into this positive environment and all the hellos and good-mornings and how-are-yous." He started as a cashier, and he would go to a main desk to see which till he'd been assigned to each day. "It was always preceded with maybe a minute-long conversation of, how are you, how's school, what's going on, your schedule working out well? That was always a reinforcement of what's special here—and it's never stopped."

A known fact to everyone who works there is that people are invited into Wegmans to do good and to be nice people. They are given resources and training to do their work, and they are invited into membership in the group with the belief that they can and will do good things. And so, many of the people who work at Wegmans gladly are active followers, because in following they get to do good—to help people, to smile, to enjoy each other's company, support their community, and contribute to a very successful business. They become connected to each other in a workplace that thrives on the experience of enjoying the people around them. "That's how most of our people come to us," said CEO Danny Wegman. "They visit our store and say, 'I like this. I'd like to be part of this,' and that's the really wonderful part about it, whether you are fourteen or eighty."

Danny and President Colleen Wegman visit different stores every Saturday to talk with people—employees and customers—and continue to make connections. Jack DePeters, Wegmans senior vice-president of operations, also makes connections during store visits. Gerry Pierce, a thirty-six-year Wegmans employee who now has responsibility for human resources across all stores and corporate offices, speaks admiringly of store visits with DePeters. "[Jack will] be walking around and noticing what he should notice—what the lines on the front end look like, what the merchandising looks like. Then he'll see an employee down the aisle, and he'll walk down there and just go over and say, 'How are you doing?' Not 'What are you doing?' but 'How are you doing?' And shakes his hand. That makes that employee feel special: 'That's one of my leaders, he just came down the aisle just to say hi to me.'" The connection happens because it is sincere and natural, and the action that reinforces the connection—saying hello, asking how someone is doing—is understood to be important.

According to Danny, Wegmans has always valued connection, from the time of the company's inception. And they also spend time reinforcing it in how they operate the business, as the nature of the store visits indicate. The act of helping people who follow to understand that who they are and what they do is valuable is not an earth-shattering secret to success—yet it is a more challenging activity than many of the sophisticated employee relations, customer service, or strategic engagement initiatives that exist in many organizations, because it is real. It is challenging because in order for a person to understand that he or she is valuable, the connection must be sincere and honest.

When the example set by leaders *is* sincere and honest, it all works. Connections spread throughout the rest of the organization, and to customers as well. And the benefits are tremendous, because people want to come to work and want to help each other. Customers want to come to the stores, and they get great service. And there is also a long waiting list of communities that would love to have Wegmans open a grocery store in their area—not just for the quality of the products but also for the quality of the workplace experience that people in the community would have access to. As an example, at the newest Wegmans store in Prince George's County, Maryland, 600 of the 650 store employees were hired from the local community.

"I think that it starts from the top," said Farr. "If we get visits from our corporate leadership, it always starts with, 'How are you, how are things, are things going well?' It always begins with that. And it ends with that. Our day around this table always starts with asking our folks how they are doing. Then we get down to business. We do those things exceptionally well, and it keeps it going."

It does keep going—straight out to customers, who feel a connection to the cashiers, the department managers, the stores, the whole company. That Wegmans store that just opened in Prince George's County in October 2010? They had 1,500 people waiting outside to get in on opening day—with some people arriving as early as 4 A.M. to be first to enter the new store. That's a true customer connection!

As Jack DePeters says, "We have one simple rule: incredible service. That's everywhere. A brand-new employee today can feel good about giving incredible service. They are empowered to let no customer leave our store unhappy. It's a simple message. . . . Nobody leaves without a smile—a smile makes a big difference." In 2005, when Wegmans was awarded the top spot on the 100 Best List, DePeters joked that they were a $3 billion company being run by teenaged cashiers —an observation that raised some eyebrows. But at the end of the day, he said, it's

> I think that you really form quite a camaraderie with the folks you work with. There are networks that you form with people, be it in your department or in the programs you are working on. You spend a lot of time with people so they become your sounding board, people who are there for you and care for you and carry you through so many different things in your life.
> —*Wegmans employee*

the truth. "And if you don't get it, then you don't know the job of that front end," he said. "Because that is where the customer is transacting their money. That's where they are giving you the hard green. And you better be doing it right."

NOT CONVENTIONAL WISDOM

The practices that enable leaders to value followership run counter to much of the leadership and management wisdom about how to get ahead and beat the competition. Convention holds that leaders occupy an elite position, thinking of strategy and unique competitive formulas, setting out sophisticated protocols. The practices described in this chapter, in contrast, place emphasis on the sophistication of relating to employees. I'm not suggesting that conventional wisdom is all wrong— merely that the total package is out of balance. Many leaders place too much emphasis on strategy and market share, to the exclusion of attention to employees and culture. And the proof of the need to elevate employees and culture to the same level as other significant issues lies in the fact that each of the companies in this chapter is beating their competition. Significantly.

At Gore, they cite as one of their competitive advantages the clarity with which leaders can move forward because they have been chosen by their followers. At CH2M HILL, they cite their culture of accompaniment as something that translates to a better customer experience. And at Wegmans, they say that their success is due to the fact that they have created a positive environment where people want to spend their time—where everyone feels connected.

Leadership in each of these companies is not a position but an activity. Trustworthy Leaders understand that it is their actions that convey their ability to lead, not the placeholder they may have in an organization chart. Followers will reflect their leaders and challenge their leaders to be better. If leaders are open and honest, chances are followers will be, too. If leaders ask good questions and try to get people involved in finding solutions and creating new options, then followers will do that, too. Yet if leaders are concerned only with their status and position, well, followers will follow. It all depends on what followers are invited into when they join.

In great workplaces with Trustworthy Leaders, the separation of the needs of the leaders from the needs of the followers is minimized, if not completely eliminated. Excuses are not made for leader behavior that harms followers—such behavior is simply something that every leader commits to avoid. There's a lot of hand-wringing in leadership literature these days about how a leader can possibly do all the important things she was hired to do and also pay attention to the needs of her followers. This concern rings hollow. There is nothing disjointed between the actions of Trustworthy Leaders when they are leading externally or internally, because they are always thinking of the followers. That is part and parcel of how they lead, how they successfully implement their strategy, pursue goals, and create a great workplace. The leader is not separate from the group; he or she is a member of the group—and the comments of the leaders and followers shared here affirm this very basic element of Trustworthy Leadership.

CONTINUING THE CIRCLE

Although all of the elements of a Trustworthy Leader's Virtuous Circle are connected and influence each other, the active engagement of followers serves as the first step that Trustworthy Leaders will take outside of their personal stance on leadership. That is, a sense of honor and commitment to inclusion are first developed through the powerful experiences and deeply held personal beliefs of leaders. Valuing followership is the first step on the Trustworthy Leader's journey, in which the leader takes what is deeply held and seeks to make it visible.

Engagement and interaction with followers requires that a leader move into that stage of his or her development in which leadership actions will be tested daily. So with honor and inclusion as a guide, followership means opening the door, talking with people, and asking them to join you.

In the next chapter we'll focus on another important leadership action that helps to build trust and strengthen followership—sharing information. Great leaders build trust with followers by giving them access to information in ways that enable them to be successful. This continues the process of creating a Virtuous Circle of Trustworthy Leadership.

The Roots of Valuing Followership

Terri Kelly became president and CEO of W. L. Gore & Associates in April 2005, having served prior to that as a divisional leader of Gore's Fabrics Division. In a September 2005 interview with *Fast Company* magazine, in which she was labeled the "Un-CEO," Kelly spoke of the need for leaders to be self-aware, to understand their flaws and their impact on others. She told of an important early encounter she had with company founders Bill and Vieve Gore. The incident harks back to the sense of humility inherent in the leader's role, as well as the opportunity for connection that this creates with followers. "Early in my career," she said, "when I was hired as a new engineer, Bill and Vieve Gore invited me to their house for a cookout and pool party. Bill was the one flipping the burgers."

Although that was a nice encounter and certainly conveyed humility and equality in the leader-follower relationship, it was just an introduction. As Kelly says, "Having grown up in the company, there's no doubt that I've been shaped and molded by the culture. Those values were instilled in me at a very early stage in my career. I had the good fortune to know the Gore family, to get to work with them, so I understood firsthand what this is all about—I was a part of it in action. That has helped me navigate different leadership roles. And here at Gore you're really put to the test of matching what you'd like to do from the business perspective with how it matches the culture so there's consistency. I think the biggest thing I bring is a respect for the culture, as well as an appreciation of the need to steward it."

Kelly always tells the associates that they need to be part of stewarding and investing in the culture as much as they do in product innovation. "You cannot just let it drift," she says. "The trick is not to have us live in the past.

There's value to having our associates appreciate how rich and deep this culture is, and it's genuine all the way back to our founders. What I've found, though, is if you stop there, they want to go back fifty years. That's not going to help the business. Our business is different. It was smaller then, things were less complex, a lot of the business was conducted locally—and that world doesn't exist anymore."

Now they spend time talking with new associates about the values of the founders, showing videos, and telling stories about the early days. Yet very quickly they shift gears to what role the associates play as stewards of the culture. This is part of the effort to shift ownership for the culture to the associates. As Kelly says, "Ultimately, yes, I play an important role, but if we don't have every associate feeling that same connection, it's not going to work. It's fundamental to our philosophy that we're distributing leadership and ownership out to 8,500 associates."

Kelly's early encounters with the Gores had a significant influence on her understanding of the importance of choice in both leading and following. In part because of the humility shown in Bill's willingness to cook for a new associate, and the respect that was conveyed to her as a new associate by the invitation to join as a fully valued and valuable contributor, Kelly chose to follow Bill and Vieve. And the difference in work quality when choice is a factor is something she believes in very deeply. Kelly has spoken often of the commitment at Gore to how things get done, not just what gets done. Although she finds that this places a particular responsibility on people in leadership positions, she also sees it as simply one of the elements of making a commitment to be a leader. Some may believe that it would be easier for a leader to simply tell people "Just do it," yet Kelly believes that in the long run a leader will be much more successful if people act because of their commitment to the leader and the process rather than because of an order to do something.

CHAPTER FIVE

SHARING INFORMATION

Most of us have heard the saying "Information is power" at some point in our working lives. Employees may utter the phrase in frustration when they feel their leaders or managers are withholding information in order to keep a hold on their power. Or it can explain why, when you ask for information, the other person suddenly becomes reluctant to share. It also affirms why so many companies have entered the information discovery and sharing business—information is powerful, valuable, and useful.

Games of hide-and-seek inside organizations in which information is the bait are some of the most destructive and least successful corporate practices, given the radical shifts in access to information that have occurred over the past decade. They consume significant amounts of time and energy, divert people from their collective contributions to the organization, and cause great harm to a leader seeking to be seen as trustworthy.

Given the benefits of sharing information in the right way and the drawbacks of withholding it, it stands to reason that leaders who want to be seen as trustworthy *must* figure out effective ways of sharing information. Two-way communication—sharing information, receiving feedback, and sharing information again—is absolutely critical to the development of trust.

Many of the practical tools used for sharing information—such as newsletters, staff meetings, and email blasts—can be easily identified and implemented within most organizations. Sharing information with people via email or bulletins posted on company notice boards, for example, is easy and practical. Yet precisely because whipping out that email and sending it to 150 people simultaneously is so easy, the tactic can be overused.

A few years ago on a consulting assignment, I was waiting with a group of employees to begin a focus group interview. The conversation turned to people's displeasure with the volume of email announcements they were all getting. One woman looked up at the group with a sly smile and said, "That used to be a problem for me, but I've figured out a great way to take care of that." Curious to know her approach, her coworkers waited to hear more. "It's easy," she said. "Anything I haven't gotten to by the end of the day on Friday just gets deleted! Yep, I just zip up that whole bunch of emails, announcements, meeting reports, important reminders, and it all goes in the trash. And I make sure I empty the trash right then. It feels really great to leave for the weekend knowing that when I come in on Monday morning, my inbox will be empty!" Everyone around the table cheered.

Clearly all the people who had been sending this woman email had taken advantage of one of the practical tools available for information sharing. Yet too much information was being shared, and the woman receiving it, because of the sheer volume of what she received, had lost her attachment to anything in it that might have been useful.

Trustworthy Leaders use a more profound set of tools to create two-way communication as they seek not only to provide information to people but also to share it in ways that enable people to use it. These tools are more powerful in their impact, yet harder to see. And they make all the difference in great workplaces.

As a Trustworthy Leader, you must go beyond the practical tools like mass email and tap into the profound. And what that means is tapping into *why* you want to share the information in the first place. Which takes you back to the Virtuous Circle—to your sense of honor, inclusion, and followership.

Humility, reciprocity, and position awareness—the hallmarks of leading with honor—guide your openness and transparent sharing of information. As a Trustworthy Leader who is honored by your followers, you will be less likely to experience the insecurities that might drive a less Trustworthy Leader to hoard information. The mutual respect at the base of feeling honored creates a strong commitment to share information with people who you know will use that information wisely.

A commitment to inclusion is also an important tool when sharing information. It helps you to create a place in the sharing process for question and answer time, feedback, and evaluations of the message content. Inclusion affirms your appreciation of others' need for the information, and by openly sharing, you ensure that everyone has been fully included in the process.

Finally, engaging followers serves as a profound tool because Trustworthy Leaders who value their followers know that in order for those followers to be successful, they need information. As described in Chapter Four, an important step in establishing a trust-based leader-follower relationship comes from acknowledging that a person's choice to follow is made not from an expectation of compliance with an edict or job requirement. And a well-informed person will be in a better position to make the positive choice to follow you than would a poorly informed person. Sharing information is a critical part of the invitation for someone to make that choice.

Information sharing practices that rest on a leader's sense of honor, practice of inclusion, and respect for followership distinguish the greater success of Trustworthy Leaders from those leaders who simply stop at doing what is practical, like sending out lots of email or posting an abundance of company notices. The use of the practical combined with the profound always fuels the actions of Trustworthy Leaders. It creates the unique mix of activity that binds giver and receiver in an overlay of trust.

There are three distinct concepts that I see in the approach that Trustworthy Leaders take to sharing information.

The first concept involves sharing information to *promote understanding*—of the organization's work and its mission, and of how an individual's work fits into the larger picture. Importantly, understanding needs to be approached from the recipient's point of view. Though this may seem obvious, all too often information is shared from the perspective of the one who has the more complete story. When that happens, information-sharing can actually result in *less* understanding, rather than *more*.

The second concept concerns sharing information in ways that *enhance participation*. Practically speaking, this means ensuring that people have a mechanism for asking questions, that multiple access points are available for the shared information, and that people are asked to evaluate the effectiveness of the information sharing. Each of these actions gives people a way to participate in information sharing. Yet more can be done to actually invite participation by creating an atmosphere in which people are comfortable asking questions, know enough to be well-informed, and are asked to give feedback to continually improve the process. An invitation to participate enhances all forms of information sharing and creates an expectation that people are always welcome to contribute.

The third concept involves sharing information in such a way that it *extends influence* to people. This is the most challenging, yet it is the most critical to truly developing trust with people. When people are given the opportunity to influence the outcome of an activity, their desire to understand and the dynamics of their participation change. People feel that they have a stake in the outcome. Your job as a Trustworthy Leader is to ensure that the feeling of having a stake in the outcome is based in reality—that people really can influence the outcome of a situation. This requires some practical steps, such as inviting workers to participate in meetings in which outcome decisions will be made and making sure they are well-informed so that they understand the issues. Beyond that, extending influence requires that you let go of your position power, and that you deeply listen to what other people have to say, as an indication of your openness to being influenced.

These three concepts—promoting understanding, enhancing participation, and extending influence—are combined in the information sharing practices of great leaders and serve as one more way of showing people that you are trustworthy. In the rest of this chapter, you'll see how you can create your own combinations of practical and profound practices as you share information with others.

PROMOTING UNDERSTANDING

Understanding does not come from simply hearing information or from receiving an email in your inbox. There is always a necessary additional phase after the information comes in: time for questions and answers, time to ensure that people understand the information shared. This loop—whether it happens through a feedback session, Q&A, or discussion—is a critical part of the process of information sharing that promotes understanding. This should also all be based on what I would characterize as a philosophy about information sharing: an approach based in both the value of information and the value of people.

At Scripps Health Care, Vic Buzachero—corporate senior vice president of Innovation, Human Resources, and Performance Management—has a rich appreciation for the importance of information sharing. He calls his approach to the task one of "communication and alignment"—one in which he seeks to share information with people in their own "language," on their own terms, so that they can use it. Buzachero wants to ensure that as many people as possible both receive information and understand it. His approach at Scripps Health serves as a valuable example for any leader seeking to take this first step.

"If you are the finance officer," he explains, "you don't jump up in the middle of a meeting and say, 'Okay, we are going to put together a budget where the capital plan is going to have a capital asset pricing model in it, and we are going to have the following hurdle rates for capital,' etc. People's eyes will glaze over." The operations people in the meeting, he warns, will be worried about how production is going and what supplies they need and how to keep the business running. The finance officer's pronouncements will just slide by. "So what does a good finance person do?" he asks. "Translates all the financial information to create value for the operating people so that they can sit down and go through the information together. In my area of human resources, we have our own responsibility to translate all the people information for others to ensure that leaders can use it to guide their actions. We need to step out of our own language as well and speak to others so they can understand us." Much of Buzachero's work is in HR, but this need for translating is universal. *All leaders*, no matter the department, need to take the particular information related to their area of expertise and translate it so that it can be understood by others. Only then will it have the potential to be useful.

Even well-intentioned managers can diminish their impact when they don't spend the time necessary to translate their message. Buzachero posits that this happens because they're too busy either defending their work or feeling insulted that people don't get what they're saying. "Well, no, they won't get it initially," said Buzachero; hence the need to be multilingual. "Your role is to translate your expertise to the board members and senior executives, and to all levels, to simplify and clarify it as much as possible. And you have to translate it on their terms, not your terms." It's the job of any leader who wants to be understood, and is not a question of dumbing down or simplifying to the point that a four-year-old would understand it, which would be insulting. Yet it is absolutely critical to take the information you have and move it out of the special language that often develops within a profession or practice area—to translate.

Not that doing so is easy. It's very natural to talk to others from your own vantage point. "I have gone through the mistakes of translating things on my terms and then thought, 'Why don't you get it? That's the way we do it in HR.'" The reality, Buzachero has realized, is that the audience doesn't care about his special language. What they do care about is how the information can create value for them. Translating it takes time, and energy, but the reward is a new level of understanding.

"That's where leaders should spend their time," Buzachero said. "Making intelligence and knowledge actionable. Because that's what people want: to be able to take action and contribute to the benefit of the organization. And they can best do that if they understand what's being asked of them and what's being shared with them." Leaders need to make sure that all employees have the information necessary to do their work, and that they see the connection of their work to the larger goals of the organization. "More than other things, communication that is aligned with the mission and values of the organization is critical," Buzachero said. "One way to get the best talent to come together and deliver outstanding patient care is to have people understand how their work fits into the whole system. People will be more engaged and will trust their leaders if we help them to understand."

Once you've approached the issue from the recipient's point of view and made sure time has been allotted for clarification, you're still not done. Understanding also involves making sure the communication is in alignment with the company's actions, and Buzachero gives a great deal of attention to this. If an administrator takes the time and effort to tell employees they are

> I think we have an absolutely wonderful clinic, and the leadership has had all to do with that because they are approachable, they are not behind closed doors where you can't get to them. If you have a complaint or something good or a new idea, they are always there to support you. I think the more they give, the more their employees give. It's just great. Really great.
> —Scripps employee

important, for example, but then won't share information about business results with them, then there is a lack of alignment between what is said and what is done. When such a breach happens, it's very difficult—if not impossible—to realign and earn back the lost trust. To complicate the subject further, sometimes the lack of alignment is the result not of a person, but of a system.

"Many times," Buzachero said, "when you look at some of the processes and systems in our organizations today, it looks like the customer is the audit department, or compliance, or the IRS. Well, they are not our customer. The customer is our patient, our staff, and our managers. We have to do everything in a compliant way, but we do not build a system for compliance; we build a system for our customer. That system can get out of alignment very easily, given all the pressures we face."

In other words, though people may be told their purpose is all about the patient, that message may seem disingenuous if you spend your entire day working to please the audit department or some other oversight body. In a health care setting, as a Trustworthy Leader, you need to make the connection clear, to ensure that everyone understands how compliance *is* connected to the patient, staff, and managers, and to also keep the focus on the true customer.

Finally, sharing information so that people can understand involves a high level of transparency. "Effective communication requires eliminating barriers and being transparent. To be transparent you need to share information," Buzachero said. "Why do some decisions look out of alignment? Is management not walking its talk? Maybe people don't have all the information and management really *is* walking its talk. We always have to ask 'How can you share that information and become more transparent?'" Buzachero has shared quite a bit of information in order to be transparent, including placing himself in the hot seat at large meetings and allowing employees to ask him any question, then answering them honestly. Board members and others have expressed concern about this level of openness, fearing the release of trade secrets. But Buzachero feels that usually no one betrays the trust. "After you say, 'We trust you,' and you show that you can be trustworthy," he said, "people really appreciate the honesty."

Ultimately, it boils down to a very simple premise: if people don't understand what is going on, their ability to trust you will be compromised. If they do understand, they will be open to trusting you deeply. And that level of trust that you develop over time will make it possible to fulfill your mission quickly and effectively. Following Buzachero's example by sharing information that creates understanding will also help you to move on to the next step in the process: enabling people's ability to participate.

> For me, I think one of the best words that people are using is *transparency*. I think that is a big one for us, when you ask your manager: "When are we going to have money for this equipment?" or whatever we need, and having that person say, "I don't know" or "Not until next year," being honest is a really important thing. I think people respect the manager, even if it is bad news. A lot of other businesses do not foster a trust environment, but our leaders are very honest about what's going on.
>
> —Scripps employee

ENHANCING PARTICIPATION

People at Hoar Construction, a real estate contracting and construction firm, often describe themselves by what they are not. They are not bashful, they are not shy to speak up, and they are not passive if something has happened that they disagree with. In part because of what they are not, what they *are* is part of a very successful company with a strength of character and depth of reserve that is now propelling the company forward as the construction market—dismal in the global recession that began in 2008—begins to pick up steam.

Hoar Construction has been recognized as one of the Best Small & Medium Companies to Work For since 2007. Leaders there invite people to participate in the life of the organization, just as they do at

Scripps—by first helping people to understand. Communication at the company, which is based in Birmingham, Alabama, has been characterized by openness since its founding in 1940. In the last several years that openness has been heightened, as more opportunities have been created for people to see and talk with their leaders. This brings with it a certain level of vulnerability for leaders, because decisions can be challenged directly. Yet at Hoar, leaders believe that they—and the company—are better off if they hear people out, and they use the compliments and the criticism to make the business stronger.

At a base level, Hoar uses the same practical communication techniques many leaders do: they send out newsletters and emails, go on site visits, and join in team meetings. They do it vigilantly, and it's effective. One employee, Stacy, says, "I feel like one of the things that our upper management does is they keep an open line of communication with everyone. The economy is not great right now. I am in the Tennessee division. I'm not in Birmingham all the time, but we always feel like we know what's going on down here because we have regular updates from the president of our company, and state of the economy updates. We know what big jobs have been awarded down here. I feel they do a very good job of keeping everybody in the know."

Yet there is also something more that happens at Hoar, something that goes beyond the base level and underscores leaders' willingness to share considerable information and answer innumerable questions. Namely, the Trustworthy Leaders at Hoar want people to understand the information being shared, and they want people to *use* it—to ask more questions, pursue a new idea, or find inspiration to take action. Leaders take the time to visit with employees, to find out what they're doing, to answer questions and ask questions of their own. They promote participation by example. So the leaders are not only sending the emails and messages Stacy finds so valuable but also sharing those messages in person. As another employee, Frank, says, "Being a construction company, we have many job sites that are out of state or out of the county. Our upper management travels to those sites to keep in touch. Not only do they invite you to come in and talk to them, but they come to keep in touch with the field. It's not unusual to look up and see [CEO] Rob Burton at your side or [COO] Steve McCord. They come down and they keep in touch with what's going on."

All this contact with leaders who make it a point to visit with people, ask questions, and involve themselves in discussions with employees at job sites inspires those same employees, in turn, to participate in other discussions and activities. Participation is said to be essential to the success of the organization; it supports the development of trust between employees and managers, leaders, and followers. To this end, I share two specific examples that illustrate the effectiveness of the invitations that come from the Trustworthy Leaders at Hoar and the benefits that the company is able to reap from people's participation.

The first is a simple act: the publication and widespread distribution of "Lessons Learned" memos to all employees. These memos are prepared after an individual or a project team addresses a difficult situation. The memos are created by the people involved in resolving the challenge, and they are posted on the intranet for everyone to see. The people involved may also be asked to teach a class at Hoar University (the company's internal resource for all training and development courses) to address the very problems they faced, so that others might avoid such problems in the future.

"Lessons Learned" is a step more formal than the question-and-answer sessions that happen regularly on job sites and in staff meetings, yet the memos take their inspiration from the same source: the belief that people at Hoar want to do good work and always want to get better. Leaders share a deep respect for people's ability to absorb information and turn it into useful knowledge. "Lessons Learned" offers a very practical example of a way that information is shared and people are invited to participate. It also affirms the profound respect that leaders have for everyone in the business. Leaders trust that people will use the information provided to them wisely, and they make multiple efforts to invite people into the process of information sharing.

A second example is more expansive; it involves Hoar's ongoing training programs. The company takes a broad view of training, sharing information not only about how to pour cement and other technicalities of their work but also about *how to participate effectively* in the life of the organization. There are very clear strategic reasons for this emphasis. "If you think about what you do on a construction job site," says the company's vice president, Douglas Eckert, "at times we've got twenty partners and subcontractors, many of them new. We don't know them. We have to all get along, and we have to all build this building that's never been built before and figure it out. You have to be incredibly optimistic, and you have to be very well-trained. But one of the things you have to do is, you have to be able to deal with people and problems that come up."

To this end, Hoar trains people on conflict management and on leadership skills. And then they take it even further, getting rid of any obstacle blocking the road to full participation. "We say that our people are going to perform best if everything in their lives is going well," Eckert explains. "What does that mean? Negotiation, for instance, is very important in business. But it's also important for people in their families. Those things really matter to people, so we train them to negotiate. If they can balance their own checkbook and do a great job with that, they're going to be a lot happier. So let's give them financial assistance. Let's get experts in here to help them be able to balance their checkbook and keep their family well taken care of. We do everything we can to develop the whole person. So, at the end of that experience, they are going to know how to put concrete in, they're going to know how to go to a new community and deal with people they haven't ever dealt with before, and when they get home at night, they're going to have a better relationship with their family. We take a very broad view of our responsibility and our opportunity here."

Hoar walks their talk. Not only do the leaders tell people that they want them to participate, but they also share information that teaches them how to do it. And then the leaders clear clutter from the path so that people can participate.

You can see the positive benefits of this effort clearly when challenging times come up and workers step forward. The construction industry has faced some difficult conditions, and when everyone works together to overcome the obstacles, it's richly rewarding. "Because we live in this culture and because we've succeeded together," says CEO Rob Burton, "people are also more willing to go through difficult times together. I think people are more likely to rally together, and say, 'Yeah, we understand it's difficult. What can we do to help?' I've been totally blown away with their willingness to do whatever we ask and their understanding of the difficulties in front of us."

When you share information in ways that invite participation, and when people's participation is acknowledged and respected, you continue to strengthen your Virtuous Circle of Trustworthy Leadership. Next, a leader must enable people to have influence. When added to understanding and participation, the combination is spectacular.

> One of the things about working with our managers is that none of them are unapproachable. There is an open-door policy here that I can go to the CEO of this company down to a laborer of this company, and everyone is approachable from every angle any time, whatever. That makes for a good relationship when I know that I'm welcome in the CEO's office. That's good.
>
> —Hoar employee

EXTENDING INFLUENCE

Being able to influence a situation—whether by simply being able to vote for one or more choices, or by actively arguing your point of view—raises your personal stake in the outcome. Your ideas become active during the discussion or presentation, and what comes next, the outcome, will be shaped by your contribution. Sharing information in such a way that you extend influence to people is akin to sharing power, which takes us back to the adage that "information is power." Information can be turned into knowledge—which is what gets created when people are able to work together with shared information. And knowledge is like rocket fuel.

It should come as no surprise that the folks at Google spend a lot of time sharing information, as that is a primary platform of their business: to find information and distribute it in ways that will make it accessible to the most people as quickly and easily as possible. Yet what happens externally for an organization isn't always what happens internally. Google's leaders might just as easily have come from the old-school "information is power" camp that holds on to all the power by keeping internal information hidden. Luckily for everyone who works there, that's not the case. Google's leaders are from the *new*-school "information is power" camp. They choose to share power by actively seeking ways to make information available to all, increasing every Googler's ability to influence the activities of the organization.

At Google, influence is extended as part of the culture of creating great things *together*. To ensure that people have the information they need to influence the outcome of events, Google's founders committed early on to creating an organization in which openness and transparency would be commonplace. People who succeed at Google are able to do so in part because of their ability to take in the information that is available and use it—to influence their own work, influence other projects, and influence how they interact with others and what questions they ask. When Google's leaders share information, they expect that people will be influenced by it and that they will do something, think something, or share something. In other words, information will enable people to extend their influence back to the organization.

Leaders at Google have often said that they'd rather people learn about important information from someone inside the company than from an external source. When information is shared internally, the person who shares it can be asked for more details and is held responsible for clarifying anything that might be confusing. This holds for department managers as well as for the two founders, who regularly present at the Friday afternoon TGIF gatherings. These weekly gatherings, to which everyone is invited, emphasize openness and put a premium on asking questions and giving honest answers.

The impact of the large-scale interaction in the TGIF meetings carries over to smaller group settings as well. The managers who are considered to be the best at Google are those who are the most effective at communicating—willing and able to answer questions, listen to people, and extend influence by supporting employees' efforts to create and work on their own projects. One employee described the support and freedom she receives from her manager: "My manager is there for me. He doesn't really 'manage' me in any way; he is there to help me in a very real sense. I've said no to my manager a lot more than I've said no to my teammates. We can have an open conversation, and that's really refreshing. It lets me work with my teammates to figure out what we should be doing. We are the people who know the stuff we're working on better than my manager. I think that's really unique, empowering, special, and it's something that I really cherish."

For a fuller understanding of people's ability to influence the internal workings at Google, I turn to David Fisher, the former vice president of Global Online Sales and Operations. Fisher found a culture at Google unlike that at any company he worked for previously. During his time there, he learned to be more open with information, to invite participation, and to extend influence to others.

When Fisher first started at Google, he was struck by how open people were to ideas. The pattern at his previous employers—and in many corporations in general, he says—was very different: "In places I've worked before, you have an idea and the first thing that happens is that everyone comes up with a list of why it won't work or why there's a problem." Fisher contrasted this with life at Google, which he says is much more a place in which people ask "Why not?" and seek to free each other from constraints.

He acknowledged going through a period of having to adjust to this new openness. "It took me a little while to realize that Google's answer to the perennial list of why something won't work is that we are going to absorb the risks, within limits. It's really very liberating—it's much more about trying to do things that are big and different from the way things have been done before. In some ways, precedent can become an anchor that can weigh you down if you let it."

The second difference he noticed between Google and his other employers was the lack of hierarchy. Leaders at Google talk with everyone and listen to everyone, and it starts at the top. Fisher spoke of having recently been in a meeting with cofounder Larry Page in which Page explicitly asked for input from "the people who are making the product decisions," not the executives. Fisher, who previously worked in Washington, DC, said he saw a lot of people there who thought that the title was what mattered most. At Google, it's much more that the *ideas* matter, especially the ideas from the people who are creating the product, providing the service, and interacting with the customer. And because their input is so important, they influence the outcome of decisions.

Fisher told a story on himself that both highlights how extending influence works at Google and shows his own ongoing learning as a Trustworthy Leader. "Two nights ago I drafted something for a new part of AdSense that we're trying to develop and make progress in. A key question we're facing is: What will our go-to-market strategy be for this product? I was sitting with some folks on my team who are working with me on this, and they said, 'We've got all these great people interacting with advertisers around the world. Why don't we just ask the team?'" Bingo! Fisher wrote a short note, and they set up a site where people could post their ideas and everyone could vote on them. Fisher explained, "I'm confident that there are lots of great ideas out there, but sometimes you need to invite people to submit them a little bit more. Maybe when you're a small organization, that happens a little more naturally, but here we wanted to make sure we reached everyone."

What is so interesting about Fisher's story is how it clearly illustrates the potential for people with information and experience to contribute to and influence something larger than themselves. Fisher's team members and the people interacting with advertisers around the world have a wealth of information to tap into. The process of setting up an internal website through which people at Google could respond to Fisher's query shares information with them so that they can understand the question, and invites them to participate in the process of creating a new part of the AdSense platform.

The lack of hierarchy that struck Fisher was also evident in the AdSense meeting he described. Fisher, in a hierarchy, would be at the top of the food chain. In the meeting he described, he is sitting with people on his team, and they—the team members—provide the input that leads to the decision to ask everyone else—the people in the field—for their input. Any chimera of hierarchy is blown aside as the best input is sought to answer the product question. Significantly, not only were people asked to provide input but also they were all asked to *vote* for the best option—they were invited to influence the outcome.

When you are able to approach a situation in this way, your actions as a leader will convey tremendous respect to the people whose input you seek. Your invitation to people to influence the outcome of a decision is an acknowledgment of their professional expertise. The collective voice of so many people sharing information and participating by voting will lead to the creation of unique knowledge that is likely to make the final choice much more successful in the marketplace. And the respect you show to people—members of your team and others throughout the organization who support the implementation of the product—contributes to their ability to trust you.

Google has created great power in their culture—the power that comes when you promote understanding, enhance participation, and extend influence through the sharing of information. People don't stop and second-guess themselves before asking a question or making a suggestion within their work groups or at all-company meetings. Instead, they feel empowered to contribute, and they do. One employee described the culture of openness at Google as one in which everyone has a seat at the table based on the power of their ideas, not tenure or title.

The ability of Googlers to influence the organization extends beyond their work projects to the policies and practices that affect employee life in the organization. One person spoke of recent changes that had been proposed for Google's travel policy. "They said we had to get something approved by our managers if we traveled internationally. Everyone said, 'This is ridiculous. We're just not going to do it.' [Management's] response was, 'You're right. That's ridiculous. We're going to go back to the drawing board.'"

Sharing information to extend influence reduces—if not completely eliminates—any compliance- or fear-based behavior in an organization, whether that organization is Google or any other company. If people disagree with something, they can challenge it. Because they have access to information, they can be prepared to propose something different. Well-intentioned policy changes that just don't cut it can be rethought before they become institutionalized. And rather than having people resent the fact that something has been imposed on them that they now need to accommodate, they jump in to make the situation better—they gather information and use it

> My family is from a small village in India. My parents grew up without electricity or running water, and they don't have a college education. When I go back to the village and look at the school where my mother studied, it looks the same, except for one difference: the kids in the village, through connectivity to computers and tools like Google, now have access to the same information as kids who go to Stanford. That leveling of the playing field is what Google's mission is all about. They do it in a way without worrying about profits and money. The founders and the engineers who build products are completely beholden to that idea. In many ways, everybody here is part of that one singular mission, which is the leveling of the playing field for what is now the most important resource of the century, which is information.
> —Google employee

to create a better outcome. They use their influence.

CONTINUING THE CIRCLE

Sharing information will affect how your organization is structured, what people will accomplish, and the experiences of customers and suppliers. When you share information broadly, then your organization will be less hierarchical, even if on paper there are many layers between the frontline salesperson and the CEO. Because information is necessary for the creation of knowledge, and knowledge helps people to take action, the more shared—within the context of enhancing understanding, participation, and influence—the better.

On the flip side, if people are left ignorant on key issues and their access to information is limited, that ignorance will inhibit their ability to answer questions or resolve dilemmas. Conversely, when people have useful information, they will understand more, participate more, and influence more—and be better able to meet the needs of patients, customers, and suppliers.

In Thomas Kuhn's landmark 1962 book on the history of science, *The Structure of Scientific Revolutions*, the physicist provides an elegantly simple rationale for the importance of having information broadly shared within a system, especially a system like an organization in which regular change is necessary for continued evolution: *"The reasons provided for a needed change can only appear reasonable to people who understand."* It is so simple that it can easily be missed. If people don't understand the information being shared to encourage change or pursue something new, then no matter how compelling the reasons for the change, those reasons won't make any sense. Some people may move with the change process simply because they have to—their jobs are changing. Others may try to participate yet be able to do so only to the degree that they understand the information shared.

When systemic cultural change is needed, everyone who is a part of the system needs to understand the reasons for change in order to participate and have any degree of influence during the change process. The same is true for product or service decisions. If people are asked to create a new product or provide a new service, the more involved they've been from the beginning in understanding why the new effort is being made, the better able they'll be to participate. And when they can participate, they also have the possibility of influencing. As a Trustworthy Leader, your actions can invite people in, give them the information they need to participate, and enable them to influence the outcome.

From the leaders we've just met—Vic Buzachero, who implores people to promote understanding by avoiding jargon and buzzwords and sharing information in ways that are appropriate and meaningful for the audience; leaders at Hoar Construction, who invite everyone to participate in the life of the organization; and Google's extension of influence through the continuous sharing of information with all—we see how Trustworthy Leadership moves another step forward in the Virtuous Circle while staying connected to the elements of honor, inclusion, and followership that have come before.

Some leaders, like Chris Van Gorder from Chapter Two, have a singular incident that they can cite as a turning point in their approach to leadership; others, like Bob Giles from Chapter Three, refer to a particular learning experience that caused them to see anew the power of a certain approach. Many other people become Trustworthy Leaders through a lifetime of experience. Nothing really dramatic or earth-shattering—simply the steady affirmation, over time, of a set of beliefs that is turned into action. This was the case for Vic Buzachero, who came to his philosophy about leadership and sharing information through his natural tendencies, career path, life experience, and varied interests.

Buzachero is by nature a curious person—he likes to figure things out so that he understands why something is true. And he says that he has always had an intuitive sense that people make the difference in an organization's success. "And if you intuitively know it," he says, "then you begin to try to dig in, to see how you can prove it. Some of it is proving it to yourself, and some of it is statistically demonstrating there is a difference between doing this versus doing that. It's no different than someone getting a Ph.D. and working in these areas and doing a dissertation and statistically demonstrating there

is a difference between doing this versus doing that, and it means something."
Vic took an additional step by taking those "proofs" he was developing and translating them into financial terms in ways that others could understand.

Buzachero had an academic background in finance and economics. Early on he developed the skills to take what he believed made for successful management practices and translated them into knowledge that a CFO would be able to use. His operations experience gave him an understanding of the measurements that are used to define success in many organizations—and it also gave him an awareness of the importance of collaborating with others to refine those measurements, translate them, and make them meaningful to different people in different operations roles. And his intuitive belief that people make the difference in the success of any organization provided a third key element that has supported his leadership success.

Although Buzachero's path to becoming a Trustworthy Leader is not dramatic, the impact he has been able to have on people's lives and the success of Scripps Health is. When Chris Van Gorder spoke of the reasons why he has been credited with so much success at Scripps, he cited Buzachero's contribution to the leadership team as a key reason why he, himself, has been able to accomplish so much. "A couple of years into this change effort, when I started putting together an executive team, I finally got Vic. I knew we needed to focus on the people. I went through almost a year's worth of interviews for the head of HR. I had some of the top-notch people in the country coming here, and none of them were what I wanted. Because I wanted someone who understood what we do. We are in the people busi- ness in two ways: people are our customers, and people provide all of our services. And Vic had operating experience. He understands what it takes to run an organization. It took me a long time to find him because people like him are few and far between." But Van Gorder finally did find him, and they've been moving forward ever since.

CHAPTER SIX

DEVELOPING OTHERS

I was first introduced to the idea that a workplace might be a place where a person could expect to grow personally as well as professionally almost thirty years ago, after reading the late Robert Greenleaf's "orange pamphlet" on Servant Leadership. Greenleaf, for many years the director of Management Research at AT&T, retired in 1964 and launched a new career promoting the idea that a leader should approach his or her responsibilities with an eye toward service.

Although Greenleaf is not the first person to identify the ways in which a leader's stance toward followers could affect followers' lives, Greenleaf gave significant weight to the idea that true leadership carries a responsibility to think first about being of service to others. In his essay *The Servant as Leader*, he wrote:

> The servant-leader is servant first. . . . It begins with the natural feeling that one wants to serve, to serve first. Then conscious choice brings one to aspire to lead. That person is sharply different from one who is leader first, perhaps because of the need to assuage an unusual power drive or to acquire material possessions. . . . The leader-first and the servant-first are two

113

extreme types. Between them there are shadings and blends that are part of the infinite variety of human nature.[1]

Greenleaf didn't offer specific prescriptions for how to become a servant leader. Instead, he presented a set of questions for leaders to ask themselves. His goal? To have leaders be the judge of their own success and to challenge themselves to continually strengthen their practice. He explained: "The best test [of servant leadership], and difficult to administer, is: Do those served grow as persons? Do they, while being served, become healthier, wiser, freer, more autonomous, more likely themselves to become servants?"[2]

I've seen the positive responses to these questions develop again and again from the actions of leaders at great companies. The Trustworthy Leaders in these organizations believe in supporting an individual's growth in all aspects of life, including professional development, yet they never perceive that professional activities are where development begins and ends.

Leaders in these companies subscribe to a philosophy of "developing others" that is much broader than you'll see in many organizations, and they expand the notion of development into areas often ignored elsewhere. The focus is on the whole person and what can be done to help each person learn and grow. People who work in these organizations deeply appreciate this approach, and they look forward to coming to work. Their colleagues know them as human beings first, with their work contributions just one facet of their lives. Certainly, work is tedious some days, and things don't always go smoothly, but because the work environment is open, welcoming, and encouraging, those few tedious days are seen simply as a small part of the whole experience.

As with information-sharing practices, a Trustworthy Leader's approach to developing others is based in both the practical and the profound. Although there are some leaders for whom the world is "all about me," Trustworthy Leaders aim to extend themselves to others with an outward perspective to their activities. Rather than using a self-focused lens that considers opportunities relative only to the impact on himself, a Trustworthy Leader believes his primary goal is to be of benefit to the other person. In this we see the profound commitment in the leader's approach to developing others.

Trustworthy Leaders' practical approach to developing people is born from their commitment to the organization's success. The products and services offered at any given time by an organization can guarantee its survival for only a short period of time. Trustworthy Leaders support people's acquisition of new skills, development of talents, and pursuit of opportunities that will contribute to the continued evolution and success of the organization. This commitment to organizational success is of tremendous importance, yet in great workplaces it follows from the Trustworthy Leader's profound commitment to be of service to others, rather than placing herself first. As a leader your ability to help others to learn and grow will be more effective when you start with a focus on their aspirations rather than your own.

Both the practical and profound approaches to people development are reflected in the three convictions Trustworthy Leaders hold about developing others.

The first conviction is that *people deserve the opportunity to create full lives* for themselves. This means, in part, not standing in the way of people's pursuit of their own goals, even if it means that they might leave the organization. Some of us will find fullness within the workplace, others will combine work with other activities, and all of us deserve to know that we will be supported in exploring and building a full life.

The second conviction is that *each individual is capable of many accomplishments*, and given the right circumstances, amazing creations will be realized. Efforts here focus on uncovering talents, helping people to develop or create new ones, and channeling talents towards the good of the person and the company. Leaders must see the possibilities in people and make a commitment to support their exploration and forward movement.

The third conviction is that guidance, support, and training are invaluable to growth and development, and that people and groups will be most successful when they have participated in the choice of direction for their pursuits. *Providing a path that people can choose to follow* places responsibility on both the individual, who needs to make choices, and the company, which needs to provide a path.

CREATING FULL LIVES

Griffin Hospital has created a vibrant, expansive organization through an abiding commitment to a model known in the health care industry as the Planetree approach. Planetree is a philosophy with some tenets similar to those of Servant Leadership. Planetree rests on the fundamental beliefs that everyone is valuable, that people can and should participate in their own health care, and that patient-centered care is fundamental to the success of health care initiatives throughout the world. The Planetree approach naturally flows into the conviction that every person deserves the opportunity to live a full and rich life. At Griffin, this conviction is lived out through the implementation of professional and personal development activities that help employees to explore their dreams, incorporate personal interests into the workplace where appropriate, and further their knowledge development to add depth and perspective to their ability to care for patients. Leaders are committed to supporting the growth and development of every person who works there. They have created a workplace atmosphere of openness and sharing, and they provide developmental programs that are unique not only in their industry but also among great workplaces.

"We set out to be an organization that values care giving and to value care giving you've got to value caregivers," says CEO Patrick Charmel. "That wasn't necessarily clear to us initially, as we first said we have to offer a great patient experience, and we want to provide a more holistic patient experience—and we knew that would resonate with caregivers. Yet we also came to understand early on that in order to give great care, people working here needed to be cared for." To that end, he says, "We have removed a lot of barriers that frustrate caregivers . . . we've changed systems and structures, and lo and behold, our caregivers say this is kind of a neat place to work."

So how have leaders at Griffin done it? As a starting point, they've taken the time to help caregivers understand the great value of their work. Griffin offers a week-long orientation and training program that everyone participates in when they start. The program includes an overnight experiential Planetree retreat built into the week, which provides a hint of the unique workplace opportunities to come at Griffin. The orientation makes it clear that Griffin employees will always be encouraged to pursue experiences that enable them to develop full lives, and that they will have access to a number of programs that support personal development throughout each year.

Following the Planetree messages, leaders provide active support for participation in personal development programs. One unique program is called Dare to Care, and Griffin staff members serve in the faculty role. Each month a three-hour session is spent addressing a different "action" value, so named because each value is seen as a guiding idea or concept that can be used to support the achievement of personal and professional goals. The twelve action values are Authenticity, Courage, Perseverance, Vision, Mission, Enthusiasm, Focus, Awareness, Service, Integrity, Faith, and Leadership. Charmel first offered Dare to Care as a gift to Griffin employees, one that could help them be more effective in their personal lives as well as professionally. Graduates of the program, who serve as sparkplugs to encourage others to pursue personal and professional growth, have related stories of lifestyle changes that include weight loss, smoking cessation, career goal setting, additional formal education, and personal life priority setting. The program is now in its eighth year, with eighteen "graduates" serving as facilitators. As of this writing, 367 Griffin employees—about one-third of the workforce—have participated in the personal development program.

"Imagine going through a program where every month, you take something away and are able to apply it to your life and better yourself through its philosophy," said a graduate. "I found myself applying the philosophy of the Core Action Values to my life, both personally and professionally. It wasn't until I was fully through the program that the impact it had on me was fully actualized."

"I think the 'Dare to Care' program is an eye-opener," said another graduate, "making people stop and think, 'Hey, I can make a difference in my community.' The program is very uplifting and a great confidence booster. I looked forward to going to the classes each month."

Dare to Care is a unique reflection of the Planetree philosophy and leaders' conviction that people deserve the opportunity to create full lives for themselves. And it's just one effort that encourages employees to pursue their dreams—blending personal and professional interests where possible. As a result of Dare to Care and programs like it, a number of staff members have incorporated their personal interests into the workplace—reflecting their leaders' commitment to care not only for patients but also for caregivers.

"The Planetree model of care provides the perfect opportunity for people to find a passion or interest and grow with it," says Barb Stumpo, vice president of Patient Care Services. "We had a nurse with an interest in therapeutic touch and energy and healing, and she's now a therapeutic touch specialist. We have a unit clerk who was a greyhound rescue volunteer, and she now coordinates our dog visitation program. We have Reiki masters and people in occupational health or staff nurses who have been able to incorporate their personal interests into the care services they provide." The work of Tracy Huneke, highlighted in Chapter One, provides further evidence of Griffin's commitment to encouraging people to live full lives and develop their talents.

Though Griffin's employees attend the Planetree retreat when they start working there, leaders are committed to sustaining and reinforcing the philosophy and approach over time. So, Griffin offers a one-day Planetree Renewal Retreat—*Continuing the Journey, Reaching the Summit*— to ensure that support for people's personal and professional development will always be blended, that it's not a message employees receive only during their first days. About thirty employees attend each monthly retreat. Leaders at Griffin are committed to continuing the retreats until all current employees have attended, and may keep going after that as well.

All of these activities underlie Griffin's success as an organization. Like every health care institution across the country, Griffin has faced serious economic pressures. Yet Griffin has fared better than most hospitals, with staff members contributing suggestions and offering support to keep the organization strong. In both 2007 and 2010, Griffin received the Premier Healthcare Alliance Award for Quality (AFQ)—one of twenty-three hospital winners and three health care systems nationwide to do so, putting Griffin in the top 1 percent of the nation's hospitals.

Griffin's caring environment, Planetree philosophy, and commitment to helping employees create full lives for themselves have all been created through the actions of their Trustworthy Leaders. Yet there is nothing unique about what Griffin has done that cannot be replicated in another organization. In your own organization you can create a program similar to Dare to Care that rests firmly on your own fundamental belief in people's ability to lead full lives.

> Coming here, the first thing that impressed the heck out of me is that Patrick [Charmel, CEO] came down and spent all that time with us during orientation. I worked at the executive levels my whole career, and you'd see them in the morning and you might see them at lunch, or if there was an "issue." But when Patrick came in and spent all that time with the group, and he had done his homework—he knew our backgrounds and asked questions—it was so impressive that the CEO would take that much time. That set the tone for me, and I knew then, this place really had a lot going on. Shortly after I came on board, I saw him in the parking lot. He went to shake my hand, but it was full of mud because he'd stopped to pull some weeds out! We've all seen Patrick do this stuff, and we talk about top-down management, and when you see the administration having that much ownership and care, it just all follows. You do it, too.
>
> —Griffin employee

You can also talk with people about their personal interests and how they might be incorporated into a workplace program or service. Think through what values have influenced your own personal and professional success—who helped you to develop those values? And what particular experiences challenged you to live up to them? These ideas will be the seeds for your own development of programs and practices to support people's ability to create full lives in your workplace.

EILEEN FISHER, Inc., just a short drive from Griffin, shows that a business in a completely different industry can develop an equally effective approach to developing others. In EILEEN FISHER's case, it rests on a conviction that everyone is important, has a right to learn and grow, and is capable of many accomplishments.

PURSUING MANY ACCOMPLISHMENTS

In many great workplaces, the leaders responsible for hiring will say that they "hire for attitude and train for skill." This phrase speaks to the significance of culture fit in the hiring process, and it reflects the belief that people are capable of developing the necessary skills for many areas of work. At EILEEN FISHER, a highly regarded women's clothing company, attitude is paramount in the hiring process. And as a testament to the truism of the opening phrase, the company gives employees tremendous opportunities to develop new skills and pursue multiple accomplishments.

Eileen Fisher is herself a woman of many accomplishments, with a spirit of generosity about her, so it is no surprise to find that she has created an organization in which people are encouraged to develop their talents. To create this environment, she has relied on the collaborative involvement of a team of Trustworthy Leaders who all share a fundamental belief in the value of supporting each individual's dreams and aspirations.

Although many people encounter EILEEN FISHER products in stores throughout the country, two major hubs of corporate activity are in Irvington, New York—a bucolic village on the Hudson—and in Manhattan, fueled by the hectic pace of the fashion district. These two settings seem to reflect the push and pull of the organization; there is a fast pace to the industry, the designs, and the production process, along with an effort to create a calm atmosphere in which creative minds can explore new concepts and pursue personal interests. How do the leaders at EILEEN FISHER merge the frenzy of a successful clothing company with their commitment to supporting people's growth and development? It is a balancing act that requires patience and perseverance.

At EILEEN FISHER, they place an emphasis on hiring the *person*, to ensure that their cultural foundations remain strong. This choice focuses leaders' attention on the need to create an environment in which people are motivated and persistent in their efforts to further develop their skills. Yvette Jarreau, leader of the Leadership, Learning and Development team, is one of the people responsible for creating that environment for the entire organization. Her team's recent focus has been on helping new leaders develop the skills to be insightful and observant—to see the potential in others and help them pursue their goals—with a heavy emphasis on developing people's listening and communication skills, all important culture-specific skills needed for success at EILEEN FISHER.

According to Jarreau, the development philosophy at EILEEN FISHER has been greatly influenced by Fisher's own views. "Eileen has a strong belief that you don't train people; they come to learn, and they learn from each other." People are expected to benefit from being able to share their knowledge with others and develop new ideas in a collaborative setting. "Listening to people is part of our practice here. We've developed a workshop called Conscious Listening that helps people explore and become more aware and present for each other. We created a second one called Conversations That Matter to help people think about what matters in particular conversations. We took quotes from people who have said profound things about communication and used them to stimulate conversations and help people be more effective themselves as communicators.

"One of the challenges that we've been addressing is *becoming* a leader. How do you think and make the transition from individual contributor to a leader role where you are expected to lead people and handle some individual work? The way we do it here requires a lot of selflessness. Letting go of the self and looking to the good of the whole is challenging for all of us." It is the conviction of leaders that everyone has the ability to learn and grow that ensures that the necessary time and resources are made available for these workshops.

Tenille Clyburn, who works in Visual Presentation, has been with the company for over eight years. She spoke of being the beneficiary of the culture and practices that have helped her to pursue new interests. "I feel fortunate to be here. The fashion industry is cutthroat, so being a visual coordinator at another company, I don't think I would want to. I started at the company working in Manufacturing and transferred to the Visual team. I valued the time I spent in Manufacturing, yet I realized it wasn't the best fit for me. When the internal job posting came out, I thought it would be hard to tell my leader that I wanted to transfer; I couldn't have been more wrong. She was supportive and interested not only in my growth within the company, but in my personal growth as well. Moving on to Visuals, I had no experience in the field. I'm not sure what my leader saw in me, but here I am! My passion for the brand has grown tremendously due to the openness of my leaders, as well as the opportunity for exploration in the company. If I wanted to move again, I would tell my leader. She pays attention to the things I like, and the tasks that I am given feel like they have my name written all over them. We all really pay attention to each other here."

Another person who spoke in general about her experience of leadership and development at EILEEN FISHER said, "We have leadership practices here that aren't necessarily spelled out every day, but they become intuitive after a while. Two of them are nurturing growth in yourself and nurturing growth in others. Something that I find interesting is that it's not even necessarily with the people you work with, but it's nurturing growth all around. The company understands the best use of its energy. We feed off of each other's positive energy all the time, and the results are positive. That's a really special support system that everybody understands here."

These comments reflect part of the fundamental wisdom of creating a strong culture: hiring people who fit in, and then taking advantage of the skills and interests that come with people who want to work in the organization, not just in a particular position. This is an opportunity that presents itself only when leaders deeply believe that people have multiple talents and act on their beliefs by creating an environment that supports people's ability to develop.

Many employees at EILEEN FISHER feel emboldened to try new things as a result of watching the behavior of their leaders. They know their leaders' work histories and personal interests, and they see how they've been able to move around and apply various skills to different positions in the workplace. Through this modeling, leaders extend an invitation to employees to try something new themselves.

One fifteen-year veteran of EILEEN FISHER described her experience: "I've had many different positions since I've been here. Each one evolved from taking an interest in something new. I've worked for leaders who have said, 'Your eyes really light up when you talk about that. Let's try to make more time in your job for you to develop that and work on that.' You have the basic work you have to do, but then you get to work with things you're really passionate about, and you have the opportunity to work with other groups and other teams. That's really valuable to me."

And it's really valuable to the company as well. An employee who stays with the organization means no need to recruit and train a new person. It also means that all of the personal connections that smooth the way for getting things done stay within the company. And when employees stay and thrive, the company retains a strong link to its cultural foundations. Finally, the company will have knowledgeable employees who can test out and debate new ideas internally before an effort is fully funded and implemented for the broader market. An employee who is supported by the belief that she can accomplish many things will share her innovative and creative ideas with others. This can evolve into an informal, internal research and development system that supports the growth and development of people and the organization.

This is a process Eileen herself used years ago. When the company was first started, test outfits made with new fabrics were produced on a small scale, and then everyone in the office was asked to wear the clothes to see whether they actually were comfortable and fashionable. The ones that passed this internal test would be produced for the broader market. Eileen's creative efforts benefited from the ready audience of people who were all committed to the success of the business. Their particular skills or work responsibilities were not as important as their understanding of the culture and mission of the organization and their willingness to experiment with the new clothes, supporting someone else's ability to accomplish something new and different. And it didn't happen just with new clothing designs. This approach—of trying things out internally, tapping into people's minds, asking people to participate in new ventures—is one of the great benefits that comes with a belief that people are capable of many things.

Susan Schor, chief culture officer, is the architect who puts structure and process in place to support the company's creative approach to developing others. She herself came to retail from an unlikely background in academia, in large part because of her friendship and ideological connection with Fisher. Schor's career is a great example of people's ability to apply their knowledge to new areas, as she moved from the university to the workplace in a fairly smooth transition. Still, she has faced challenges in putting her beliefs about the importance of collaborative, open, experimental environments into practice. The immediacy of deadlines, order changes, supply chain mix-ups, and other such events that regularly seem to appear in a design, manufacturing, and production company have not skipped over EILEEN FISHER.

One of the concepts Schor espouses is learning by doing. This necessitates a collaborative environment, as the "doing" part of the learning process involves teaching others what you know or willingly engaging in a learning process together so that all participants are learning and doing together. This provides tremendous benefits in terms of exposing people to new ideas that they might use for their own growth and development, but it's not always easy to get multiple people involved in thinking through each opportunity.

To address the challenges of the "learning by doing" process, leaders at EILEEN FISHER took a number of practical steps to develop their own collaborative skills, and to maintain a focus on pursuing new ideas and interests. Schor explained, "We developed a group called Leadership Forum to serve as a discussion and decision-making body. We had this belief that collaboration was right, that thinking together and bringing together the right group of people would be the foundation of our success and was most aligned with our values." Initially, some leaders at EILEEN FISHER looked at the idea of Leadership Forum as a messy, unformed system. There was no prescribed picture of how it was supposed to be, and there were few examples in either the business world or academic literature to provide a solid model of how to successfully make leadership decisions in a truly collaborative environment. Yet everyone was committed to trying something different that they believed spoke to a special and unique quality of the organization. They also deeply believed that a collaborative decision-making process for leaders would help them to be creative and thoughtful and to develop new skills that would allow them to accomplish more together than any one of them could individually.

As part of the development process for leaders, each member of Leadership Forum is coupled with an outside coach. The primary purpose of the coach is to work with each leader on subjects related to EILEEN FISHER's mission and culture, to serve as a sounding board for various situations, and to provide support as each leader creates her own leadership team within her area. As Schor explained, coaches are asked to help leaders "foster growth and development that is very 'EILEEN FISHER-ish' in their own leadership team so that these new leaders can deepen in their current areas and across the company."

Khaja Khateeb, director of EILEEN FISHER's Distribution Center, has benefited from EILEEN FISHER's culture and given back as well. Khateeb came to the company twenty years ago when he was searching for a job in the fashion industry. When he walked into the offices for an interview, he was told that unfortunately the position he was interested in had already been filled. The person who came to give him this news apologized for the inconvenience, yet invited him to stay for a conversation about his interests. As Khateeb said, "It was too hot outside to leave, so I stayed to have a talk. Our meeting ended up being an hour and a half long. Two days later, I got a phone call from her and she asked if I was interested in a job. At the time, I had three other job offers."

Khateeb spoke with his wife about his interest in EILEEN FISHER. Her concern was with the size of the company, which was very small relative to the other ones offering him work. Would EILEEN FISHER be able to offer him the same growth opportunities? Yet Khateeb felt that everything EILEEN FISHER was doing was right for a business to be successful, and, given that, it followed that he himself would be successful there. Khateeb took the position and now, two decades later, has proven himself capable of great things. He has grown from managing wholesale distribution to taking on retail and e-commerce as well, and from starting with a staff of five to now having over seventy people within his area of responsibility. It was EILEEN FISHER's approach to developing people that hooked him in the first place, and that same approach has kept him loyal. "I used to get calls from headhunters to come and work at other companies," he said. "In one of my interviews, the interviewer said to me that they are looking for someone who 'gets productivity.' In the first three months that I was going to be with the company, they said they wanted to get complaints from staff that I'm a slave driver. I told them that I am the wrong person."

The Virtuous Circle of Trustworthy Leadership continues for Khateeb; not only has he expanded his own leadership skills, but he's also taken an active role in developing others. "I've learned a lot here," he says. "It's not just managing by wandering around, it's much more than that. . . . You help people to grow personally and professionally, and they will help you. That is what happened to me at EILEEN FISHER and now I can help others. Half of my job is making sure that we are doing the work, and the other half of it is to help anyone who comes to me. People who you help will become your best employees."

Many of the workplace practices at EILEEN FISHER are unique to their culture. Although the specifics may not apply to your particular organization or leadership situation, there is much that all of us can learn from their process. First, Eileen Fisher, as the leader and founder of the organization, used her own values and beliefs as a guide for creating the culture of her organization—and she stuck by those values and beliefs when implementing programs that were out of the ordinary in the business world. Second, new leaders recruited to join the organization, who were attracted in part because of their connection to the culture, were able to provide process

---

Working at EILEEN FISHER, I have been able to pursue some dreams and grow as a person because of the things that were available to me. I started out here as Carol Gazzetta, but because of being here, I became Carol Gazzetta the jewelry designer, Carol Gazzetta the card manufacturer, Carol Gazzetta the potter, Carol Gazzetta the journalist, and Carol Gazzetta the fashion plate because I have all of these beautiful clothes. Now I can say Carol Gazzetta, the world traveler. There are so many different things that because of being in this company, I have been able to obtain, and I never would have if I wasn't here.

—*EILEEN FISHER employee Carol Gazzetta*

and structure that has helped the organization grow—and still maintain a strong hold on the founding cultural values.

The programs at EILEEN FISHER that support people's ability to pursue growth and development have themselves grown and changed as the organization has evolved. Yet throughout these changes, leaders have always carried forward their initial commitment to the idea that people are capable of many accomplishments.

PROVIDING A PATH TO FOLLOW

It's fun to visit a Stew Leonard's store. There's always someone smiling and ready to greet you, and delicious smells and attractive food displays fill the space. Customers enjoy the time in the store as well as the good food taken home. Yet what if you work there? You might think it would be hard to be cheerful and attentive all the time for all the customers— especially given that the only rule that exists at Stew Leonard's is "The customer is always right."

I've followed this organization for many, many years, and have always noticed one of their secrets to ensuring the positive customer experience: the leaders have made an intense behind-the-scenes com- mitment to support Team Members' growth and development. Team Members serve customers with confidence and enthusiasm because their own value, both personal and professional, is reinforced every day in their interactions with leaders, managers, and coworkers. People employed by Stew Leonard's surely have days when the frustration tops the enjoyment—everyone has those days—yet when everything is con- sidered, Stew's is a great place to come to work.

Many years ago, when Stew Leonard's was still just one store with a small number of employees, professional development opportunities came quickly simply because the store was growing; everyone pitched in however they could. With more stores came more opportunities, and people's career paths were naturally varied. Career path planning tended to follow the same natural growth pattern as did people's early careers. Yet during the past few years, to ensure that everyone is aware of what career opportunities are ahead of them, Stew Leonard's people-development staff has focused on creating, documenting, and sharing career plans with everyone—providing people with paths they can choose to follow.

Providing a clear path for growth is the main focus of this section, yet it's worth noticing that the Trustworthy Leaders at Stew Leonard's also embrace this chapter's first two convictions: that everyone deserves the opportunity to create a full life, and that everyone is capable of many accomplishments. Put all together, a commitment to developing others is a notable strength of the company's leaders. This commitment reaps rewards for the business, which can easily be seen in the longevity of its Team Members.

Wendy Febbraio started at Stew's in 1982 as a cashier. Now she's the training manager for frontline Team Members through Team Leaders, and she's also the assistant dean of Stew Leonard's University. Her intention was never to be a career Stew's Team Member, and the fact that her tenure there has lasted three decades is a testament to what she's received from the company.

"The reason that I picked Stew Leonard's," she says, "was because my husband and I lived across the street and I needed a place I could walk to. Stew Leonard's offered flexible schedules, we had two babies at home, and I started as a cashier."

Febbraio's original thoughts of becoming a midwife changed because of the people she met at Stew Leonard's and the growth opportunities presented to her. "I did all the jobs within the cashier department," she says. "Twenty-six years ago I wrote the training manual—the first training manual for the front end—because I thought we should have some consistency between what I said and others said. I went to the customer service desk and learned that area; I worked in the back in the money room for a couple of years counting the receipts. . . . Then I came back out to the front end as the assistant director, and from there I applied for a position within the people department to work with payroll. I came upstairs to the HR department twenty-one years ago . . ." Febbraio has managed insurance claims, run payroll, handled workers comp claims, and developed employee orientation programs. For the past six years she has been the training manager.

From the outset, it's not easy to envision a career plan that looks like Febbraio's. Yet because of her experience, and the experiences of those around her, every position at Stew's now has a career ladder, showing people what they can do to move on to new positions within the organization. The training needs are detailed, expected knowledge accounted for, success markers spelled out, and electives are even suggested that could enhance someone's skills. Staff meet with their managers to develop an estimated time frame for the accomplishment of career development steps, with regular meetings scheduled to help keep people moving forward. When you start as a cashier at Stew's, you know what to do to move on to becoming, say, a merchandiser/receiver, then a wine advisor, and then a wine administrator—potentially moving up to a manager position if that's what makes sense for you. The path is there, the training available, your manager and others provide support and guidance, and you make choices along the way.

Like Febbraio, Ellen Story also has a career history with Stew's that goes back to the 1980s. Currently the Human Resources manager for the Yonkers store and director of Leadership Development for the company overall, Story started as a cashier in high school in 1986. She was one of the first to receive a Stew Leonard's college scholarship, which enabled her to go to the College of William and Mary in Virginia. And as with Febbraio, though Story had no intention of making a career with the company, that's exactly what happened.

"I went down to Virginia yet came back and worked at Stew's during all my college vacations, whether it was Thanksgiving weekend or all summer long. During one of those summers, I helped out in Human Resources, and then before my last year I was offered a full-time position for after graduation," she says. "I had no idea really of the value of something like that, yet as I got closer to the end of the school year and all my friends were trying to figure out what they were going to do, I realized 'That's something!'"

Story assumed she would work at Stew Leonard's for a few years before finding her "real" job. But decades later, she remains at Stew's, happily. "When we opened up the new store in Yonkers, I was offered the Human Resources management position. I've been there for the last ten years, but in that time, like a lot of people at Stew Leonard's, I've helped out in a lot of different areas. We started our wine business in the Yonkers store ten years ago, so I helped out with that, which started a personal passion of my own for wine. Stew Leonard's has given me the opportunity to develop wine training programs for other staff members, and I also helped out in the meat department, of all places. I did that for about a year—from an operational perspective, learning sales practices, and all about perishable products, that sort of thing."

Two people; two stories of learning and growing on an open path. And Stew Leonard's has benefited tremendously as well. Story's experiences—especially her operational experiences working in the wine and meat departments—have been of tremendous benefit to her work in human resources. "Having the operations on-the-floor experience really engendered a sympathetic attitude toward what frontline staff have to deal with," she says. "If we're pushing down training programs—which we feel very passionate about, obviously, as we recognize the value in doing them—what we have to recognize as well is that the managers and the people on the store floor have to balance so much. Although [human resources training] is something we think is so important—stop everything, drop everything, and send people to the training room—they still have to cut fillets and grind meat. I have a definite appreciation for communicating often, as far in advance as possible, soliciting feedback to know what's going to be the most valuable program to offer them and really reinforce the whole idea that we are here to support them so they can generate the sales to keep the business running."

The positive experience of moving through positions, with training for skill and knowledge development provided along the way, is of great benefit to the individual recipients and has served as a model for the ongoing development of others. Although both Febbraio and Story followed "self-made" career paths, the current use of career ladders, training plans, and checklists gives people a head start on considering what their options might be for six months to six years down the road. And in the spirit of an intense commitment to the belief that everyone can grow and develop, some of the first career ladder diagrams that were created were for the cashiers and frontline Team Members often ignored in other organizations. All hourly positions are identified with a ladder visual, showing Team Members what they need to know to go from one position to the next, or even to a position on a different ladder completely. "We share that with each team member," says Febbraio, "so they know what the next step is. *Where am I in my current position, have I satisfied these things, what am I missing, and if I'm just about there, what do I need to do to get to the next level?* They can see it, check things off and keep track of what's still needed."

Leaders ensure that this information is shared with everyone—not just those who might have already caught the eye of someone interested in helping them move up. Human Resources staff attend department meetings where all levels are present, and they help people to see what they've accomplished and how to identify what else they need.

At Stew Leonard's there is a tremendous focus on developing talent within the organization and helping people enhance their current skills and knowledge. Part of this is simply a very smart business strategy—if you are able to keep employees with your organization for a long time, your overall recruiting and training costs will be lower and your profits will be higher. Nothing eats away at the bottom line like a loss of investment from the recruiting, hiring, and training that walks out the door when someone leaves.

A major obstacle to career development opportunities for people in many organizations is a failure to see the potential in all of the people who work there, identifying only those with "high potential" as worthy of career development attention. This blind spot can come from a hierarchical structure that keeps leaders away from frontline employees, or it can come from an attitude that certain people and certain positions are the only ones that count. This is a horribly narrow view of the world, as it overlooks those who provide direct service—the people who tighten the screws to make sure that the million-dollar piece of equipment will work, or who answer questions from a potential customer or supplier. If these people aren't told how valuable they are, then why expect the service they provide to be that valuable either? Is that a smart business strategy? Although I often admire the commitment of hourly, low-wage workers who do the right thing, provide great service, and help out as best they can, I also often marvel at how much better things would be for everyone if someone inside their company paid attention to them and told them how important they are to the success of the organization.

At Stew Leonard's that's exactly what they do—for everybody. The career development work that goes on at Stew Leonard's rests on the fundamental belief that everyone is valuable and everyone deserves the chance to learn and grow, and that sound guidance and advice can be provided so that people can make choices. Because all employees can get the information they need to keep

One of the great things I see here are the opportunities to grow. I look around the table and everyone here has grown tremendously. I remind myself all the time of these things you never got at other companies. At my last job, I never got a thank-you note, and I worked there for eight years. When I was at other companies, I used to get yelled at for doing things that Stew encourages. I would be on the phone trying to get better quality produce, better pricing, but I was getting yelled at because I wasn't going through their systems. Here, they encourage that. They want us to do better at our jobs. You always get a thank-you for that.

—*Stew Leonard's Team Member*

moving, everyone can be identified as a potential high performer, regardless of the visibility of the employee's current position. Each person is given an opportunity. Not everyone has to take the opportunity, yet everyone is given the chance to make that choice. This approach, which also reflects many of the basic tenets of Servant Leadership, is a perfect combination of the Trustworthy Leader's blending of a practical career path with a profound belief in human value.

CONTINUING THE CIRCLE

The companies in this chapter that serve as examples of developing others couldn't be more different on the surface. Griffin Hospital (community based health services), EILEEN FISHER (women's clothing), and Stew Leonard's (dairy and grocery) represent great variety in the products and services they provide, the types of work people are asked to do, and the physical environment of the workplace. Yet they are remarkably similar in terms of their leaders' commitment to helping people learn and grow.

Leaders create what is unique and special in their organizations through this commitment, and it is embodied in a willingness to listen to people's aspirations; to stretch people by involving them in programs, meetings, and discussions that are often beyond their specific experience; and to provide guidance and encouragement as people begin to explore what might be possible for them.

The inspiration for each company's leaders came from sources as varied as their industries. Patrick Charmel found inspiration from his exposure to the Planetree philosophy of health care. This approach gave him a way to mesh his personal values with a professional approach to leadership that worked in a health care setting. Many employees are now benefiting from his leadership lessons. Susan Schor hadn't thought she'd find her place in a for-profit women's clothing business, yet there it was, right in front of her. At some level she and Eileen Fisher were both trying to do the same thing, yet in different settings. Both wanted to empower women, to create places where people could thrive, speak up, learn, and grow; and both wanted to create places where people are valued as human beings beyond the tasks they perform. And Wendy Febbraio and Ellen Story took their inspiration from inside the organization where they were working, benefiting from the practices already in place. They are now helping extend those practices to the next generation of leaders coming up.

These journeys are common to many Trustworthy Leaders—ones for whom personal values of care and concern for others guide their professional success. Although in some workplaces aspiring leaders and managers are told that care and concern do not belong in a business setting, the leaders profiled in this section and throughout this book show that putting people first actually garners more success than an approach that treats employees like widgets. When you treat people well, they will follow you, listen to you, and share valuable information in return, and they will learn and grow in ways you can't initially imagine. In short, trustworthy behavior leads to great accomplishments.

In most of the situations Trustworthy Leaders will encounter in their careers, the practices of engaging followers, sharing information, and developing others will occur smoothly. Yet there will be moments when uncertainty will dominate the situation; then leaders will need to call on the reservoir of trust they have created to help move through the ambiguity and vagaries of whatever is in front of them. Seeing opportunities in uncertainty is a particular strength of Trustworthy Leaders. They can pursue these opportunities in part because of that reservoir of trust they can turn to for help. The next chapter delves into the complexities of uncertainty and shows how three different leaders have been able to keep their organizations moving forward.

The Roots of Developing Others

Susan Schor had a safe and secure position as a tenured professor of organizational behavior, management, and leadership at Pace University before she started her career as the chief culture officer at EILEEN FISHER. Most people who achieve tenured teaching positions never leave, and many others struggle to attain the level of job security that tenure brings with it. Yet Schor chose to leave Pace and join EILEEN FISHER—for many of the exact same reasons that brought her to teaching in the first place. She wanted to have a positive impact on the world.

Growing up and being politically active in the 1960s, Schor had a front-row seat in the struggles for justice, gender equity, civil rights, and the provision of opportunities to the disenfranchised. These experiences continue to guide her actions today. "I grew up with friends and family who were very concerned about civil rights and the end of the war and women's liberation," she said. "In my family, I was a little bit more extreme in wanting to change the world, though they were definitely an influence."

Added to her family and upbringing, Schor was affected by her studies. She has degrees in child development, human development, and organizational development, all which she says have influenced her approach at EILEEN FISHER. "I've always had an interest in behavior and in people working together and understanding people and knowing that people do best when they are at their best."

Schor met Eileen Fisher at a mutual friend's party, and during their conversation they realized they had a lot in common. The vision and values Fisher had for her company were similar to Schor's concerns with equity and justice. They stayed in touch, with Fisher speaking at Schor's MBA class and Schor accompanying Fisher to work for a day. "There was a simpatico experience that we had that led to my joining her for a day when she had two critical meetings," Schor said. "I spent the day with her and talked with her afterwards. She asked if I would work with her on her leadership process and talk with her about what was happening in the company." Schor's knowledge of groups and leadership behavior, her outsider's perspective, and her shared values with Fisher all helped her to see the dynamics operating at EILEEN FISHER from a unique vantage point—distinct from that of people actively participating in the meetings.

Over a period of two years, Schor became more involved with the company's leadership, working closely with Fisher herself. "It really became clear," Schor said, "that they needed someone with my orientation in the company—that external was not going to do the trick. They needed someone to guide and deepen what Eileen valued. It had gone somewhat astray and was difficult for her. Eileen asked me if I would find the right person and help that person for a year to eighteen-month transition. It was through the process of leading the search that I said to myself, 'Susan, are you nuts? It's such a fascinating company.' It was so aligned with my commitment to equity and justice."

In her work for the company, Schor has taken inspiration from her own background and from the intentions of Eileen Fisher herself, who has always expressed her commitment to people's growth, development, and freedom to explore. Schor emphasizes that her work alone is not responsible for EILEEN FISHER's culture. "What you see now in our mission and our leadership practices are not new ideas," she said. "There is just a reframing and rewording, placing us at the right point in where we are in history. This is what has been part of Eileen's vision from the very beginning."

Schor concluded that moving into EILEEN FISHER was a unique opportunity that she could not pass up. "While I felt in my academic life I was having some influence on some students, I just saw the potential for great impact for my values in a very open, learning-oriented, accepting organization. . . . In any case, it was so appealing to be part of this organization and to be able to really make a difference, and have Eileen's support in terms of the steep hills I needed to climb. I felt very, very welcomed into the company and very excited myself. I knew that I would have an impact."

CHAPTER SEVEN

UNCERTAINTY AND OPPORTUNITY

Every leader—trustworthy or otherwise—has to face uncertainty. In the last few years especially, leaders in every industry have been on a roller coaster. It is a fact that throughout your career you too will regularly find yourself in the heart of uncertainty, making decisions when the outcome and the consequences are unknown. Seeking approval for a new product or service, trying to understand compliance practices, adjusting to shifting markets, and dealing with general economic turmoil, all bring uncertainty with them. Uncertainty is a normal part of business.

Yet making decisions when the outcome is unpredictable can be uncomfortable and nerve-wracking. When we're under pressure, our creativity and problem-solving abilities can be diminished. In an effort to find solutions or antidotes to uncertainty, we often miss seeing an opportunity—yet it is precisely in moments of uncertainty that opportunities are found.

Great leaders are always looking for opportunities. With confidence in your skills and with a highly qualified team of people to help you deal with uncertainty, your likelihood of success increases dramatically. Of course, "likely success" doesn't mean that an outcome is predictable.

It just means that whatever the outcome, it's more likely to be positive than negative. And that's what a great leader wants—to be on the positive side of the equation.

As you deal with uncertainty, you will often find yourself at a crossover point where you'll have to leap from considering several options, to making a choice, to taking action; that is, you will have to pursue one opportunity over another. *How* you find these opportunities and make your choices is critical to your organization's success and your success as a leader.

Trustworthy Leaders don't approach uncertainty by applying any one theory or strategy that promises better financial performance, a greater market share, or a chance to zap the competition. Rather, their approach to uncertainty reflects the fullness of their Virtuous Circle. Even in uncertainty, when the outcome is unpredictable, great leaders work diligently to consider options and make choices consistent with their beliefs and values. Their actions reflect their commitment to a leadership practice that flows from their trustworthiness. Their trustworthy behavior helps them move through uncertainty to the opportunities that lie beyond.

Trustworthy Leaders have an edge when dealing with uncertainty because they have developed, and seek to live by, their Virtuous Circle. Honorable leaders who include employees in the life of the organization develop a highly committed and loyal workforce. They benefit from engaged, well-informed followers who aspire to learn, grow, and contribute. So although there are no shortcuts for moving through uncertainty, a well-developed Virtuous Circle will provide you with advantages in three critical areas: addressing risk, uncovering and developing knowledge, and applying wisdom.

Uncertain situations are by definition risky: if you don't know what the outcome will be, then there's a risk that you will make choices that are unproductive or harmful to the business. When you approach uncertainty with an awareness that *risk* is part of the process—that is, when risk is not just expected but anticipated—your chances for a better outcome improve. Relying on your network—the people whose commitment you've secured by treating them with honor and inclusion—will help you to identify, develop, and share the necessary *knowledge* to make and implement the right decisions. And as a leader who continuously searches for opportunities, you will develop and apply *wisdom*—that combination of analytic skill, useful insight, and practical understanding that helps you to steer through the critical junctures that present themselves when opportunities are in front of you.

In times of uncertainty, success is never guaranteed. But if you don't address risk, access knowledge, and use your wisdom, you certainly will *not* succeed. Sometimes circumstances will require you to take immediate action. At other times, you will have the luxury to decide whether or not to pursue a unique opportunity that is just visible on the horizon. Either way, as a Trustworthy Leader, if you have created an environment in which you and your colleagues work through the rough spots together, you will be well prepared for whatever comes.

In this chapter I present three examples of Trustworthy Leaders who each faced a unique set of circumstances and handled the uncertainty differently. Reflecting on how each of these leaders applied the strength of their Virtuous Circle to situations in which risk was present, knowledge was needed, and wisdom was essential, will help you to prepare for your own journey through uncertainty to the opportunities on the other side.

MAYO CLINIC: ADDRESSING RISK

Mayo Clinic, with a home base in Rochester, Minnesota, is one of the most highly regarded health care organizations in the world. People there deal with the day-to-day uncertainty that comes with treating over half a million patients every year, yet they also deal with heightened uncertainty that shows up as risk. What's the difference? Day-to-day uncertainty may mean not knowing which trauma case will arrive at the emergency room door, which patient will have an unusual illness or condition needing treatment, or which cutting-edge protocol may be a patient's only hope. In each case of uncertainty a decision needs to be made; one response is chosen over another, and people move forward. Uncertainty that comes with the added weight of risk may come from the same roots, yet will take a different turn.

In health care settings there are risks associated with the choices being made for patients—surgery, treatment options, and various medications. At Mayo there is an additional risk associated with finding the right approach to patient care that will live up to Mayo's commitment of ensuring that the needs of the patient come first. These risks are associated with Mayo's pledge to provide health care in a setting that promotes collaboration, integration of practices across disciplines, and mutual respect for all employees. There is risk in simply managing a health care organization and trying to sincerely convey to all service providers the value of their unique contributions—especially in a world in which the superstar care provider is often singled out for exclusive praise. The combination of any of these risks with one another could raise the level of uncertainty to an untenable point.

Recently, Mayo has also faced additional risk, as efforts to change the national health care system have raised questions about how services will be provided, who will make decisions about coverage, and what level of reimbursements will be allowed. As lawmakers debate these questions, people at Mayo prepare for an uncertain future.

Yet even as these elements swirl around them, the Trustworthy Leaders at Mayo seek to remain calm and continue with their work. Chief Administrative Officer Shirley Weis identified three strategies she uses to address the risks facing Mayo—both those that are expected and those that are anticipated. Weis's approach to addressing risk is deeply rooted in the elements of her Virtuous Circle. First, she relies on the honor she experiences as a leader at Mayo, as expressed in the values she uses to guide her actions. Second, she encourages information sharing and the development of a fair culture that promotes safety and accountability in high-risk situations. Third, she has enhanced the inclusiveness of a standard decision-making model to meet the needs of high-risk situations facing Mayo Clinic. Combined, these strategies provide Weis with a road map for moving through the uncertainty associated with leading in a world-renowned health care organization.

Weis reflected on the honor and values that guide her by speaking of the personal experiences that have influenced her own approach to leadership. "Being in the ranks in other organizations and having poor supervisors who weren't giving you the straight scoop, you sensed how it felt to have someone treat you disrespectfully. As adults, you expect to have the real deal—tell me the facts and we can work it out together, as opposed to having someone try to convince you it's a certain way." The life-changing lessons that Weis has brought with her from her early workplace experiences reflect her humility, reciprocity, and position awareness. "As a leader, the only thing you have is your name and your word. If people can't trust you and what you do, it harms you as an individual, and it harms your effectiveness. I learned that early on by watching others."

In her role as a leader, guiding the organization through the uncertainty of the health care industry, her personal values influence how she interacts with Mayo's staff. "As a leader, if you want to meet [patient] needs, you have to meet the needs of the employee. The two are intertwined," she said.

Weis struck a reflective note as she spoke of times when she felt that she hadn't quite lived up to her own standards and had pushed herself to learn and improve. "You make mistakes early on, and you learn from them. You strive to be trustworthy, but at the end of the day when you review the situation, you may say, 'That didn't go so well. How can I do better next time?'" Weis understands that having a strong set of personal values is aspirational, not definitive, and in order to be effective she needs to always aim her actions toward her values—seeking consistency between the two. Situations change and people's needs change, so Weis challenges herself to apply her values to changed circumstances. Her commonsense approach is beneficial when dealing with risk, as it ensures that her actions are transparent and that trust among Weis and her colleagues and staff remains high.

Weis also brings into play the lessons she learned while growing up in Michigan, watching the auto industry downsize and people lose their jobs. "Growing up in Michigan," she said, "you either went to work out of high school in the auto industry, or you went to college to get a job in the auto industry. It breaks my heart going back to Michigan now. The auto industry is struggling. They could have made changes, and they could have intervened earlier, but they didn't. I feel strongly that I can never let that happen to Mayo Clinic. Even if I have to do tough things, we'll do tough things for the right reasons. It's kind of like tough love. . . . We've had to make changes, and we were as fair as we could be, and we openly discussed it with our staff."

Weis's words echo the depth of the honorable and inclusive stance she puts into practice. She aims to have her actions and words connected—a hallmark of strong ethical leadership that is essential for anyone who aspires to be a Trustworthy Leader. As an approach to dealing with risk, this is indispensible, as it reinforces the trust that is so necessary for moving through uncertainty.

In recent years Weis has strengthened her practice of sharing as much information as possible with all staff, answering questions directly, and continually expressing her commitment to Mayo's values. She acknowledges to staff that risk is to be expected and that the way to move through risky situations is with the same values, skills, and practices used at other times. To support people's ability to come together and participate in the discussions and decisions that need to be made, Weis supports her heightened sharing of information by cultivating a fair culture at Mayo Clinic which encourages staff to speak up to prevent risk and learn from situations where risk occurs.

"Our goal to continually learn and improve as an organization," notes Weis, "means we must all be able to reflect and ask ourselves what we can do differently next time to prevent risk."

Weis is working diligently to embed a fair accountability system within the culture of Mayo Clinic. This accountability system, combined with safety habits that all staff adopt, enhances everyone's ability to ensure patient safety and better performance in risky situations.

"We are working with our staff to build a common language, widely accepted principles, and specific practices to use that enable them to address uncertainty or risk and learn from it," said Weis. This focus on safety habits and a fair culture provides particular benefits to staff who may not have the position power needed to question a situation they believe is risky. The culture growing across Mayo Clinic puts everyone on an even playing field when it comes to patient safety or risky situations. Everyone is accountable for eliminating preventable harm. Staff who may be most vulnerable to the consequences of "risk gone bad" are encouraged to speak up and are supported by the care team, as all are collectively watching out for the patient and each other. Staff do not face risk by themselves, and leaders become aware of the risks facing others and can act upon them quickly.

As an example of how the safety habits and fair culture practices have helped, Weis shared the following analysis—which was conducted within the framework of looking to create a "fair culture" for all. One of the biggest causes of everyday risk in health care settings is poor communication during patient care. Whether it's a life-threatening situation or routine care, patients can be harmed when the wrong information is conveyed from one care provider to another. Leaders know that everyone at Mayo is committed to doing the right thing, yet when situations are tense and outcomes uncertain, communication can falter.

Ensuring that staff are comfortable speaking up in tense situations is essential for effective communication and for reducing the possibility of errors in patient care. Practices that ensure clear communication and safer transitions help to reduce risk and create a blame-free culture in which people speak freely versus a punitive culture in which people keep quiet to avoid repercussions. Staff receive standard training on how to have difficult conversations, yet having those conversations under tense circumstances is different—it's an issue of culture, and that's where the safety habits and fair culture training have helped.

Weis wanted to make sure that all leaders received feedback on their openness to questions and even challenges when placed in tense circumstances. She found that although on paper everyone at Mayo was expected to receive a performance evaluation—which would include feedback on openness to challenges and questions—in practice it wasn't happening for all leaders. "Leaders can influence whole sections of the organization," Weis said, "so of course you need to give them feedback. And that happens now." No one was blamed for the previous oversight—the problem was acknowledged, and steps were put in place to address it. Now when a difficult situation arises, when someone with less position power in the system needs to question a decision or ask for more information, the fair culture practices come into play, ensuring that the question gets asked, the concerns are heard, and ultimately the right decision is made.

The fair accountability system evolving across Mayo Clinic provides a framework for having conversations so that the risks involved in various situations can be minimized. It helps to uncover relationships between workplace practices and risk, and it identifies programs—some already in place—that could be better used to reduce risk. "In those handful of situations where a staff member is willfully negligent or doing harmful things, you have to handle that, and if it's a fair culture where you can talk openly, then we can talk about the issues at hand, we can put everything on the table," Weis said. "It's picked up a fair amount of steam so far. And we know the tone at the top makes the difference. You have to be truthful and set that tone for people to really feel it is safe and fair."

Looking closely at Weis's commitment to creating a fair culture, you can see her Virtuous Circle at work. She engages followers, information is shared with all, and people develop new skills and abilities through the training programs offered. An added benefit of creating a fair culture is that the strong ethical culture of Mayo Clinic, and the commitment to Trustworthy Leadership, are reinforced as well, which helps to minimize the negative consequences the might arise in risky situations.

The third element of Weis's approach to addressing risk uses inclusiveness in decision making and supports a person's ability to challenge a decision as a devil's advocate or, in some cases, to actually veto the decision. This element stems from a responsibility charting approach to decision making used in many industries. Although most approaches to decision making assign people to one of four roles—responsible, accountable, consult, inform (RACI)—Weis customized her approach for situations in which significant risks might arise. "Everybody else uses RACI as a guide for decision making. We Mayo-ized it so we have ARCIVD—we added 'veto' and 'devil's advocate' roles. This gives the added ability for someone to speak up with concerns—to be the devil's advocate. For big projects, we put the devil's advocate and veto responsibilities in as part of the project charter and assign roles to people based on ARCIVD."

This decision-making methodology has a very practical element to it, similar to the approach to creating a fair culture. Roles and responsibilities are clear, and people are tasked with upholding their specific area. The person who is *responsible* for making the decision needs to do just that—make the decision and hold responsibility for its soundness and applicability. The people who need to be *consulted* need to ensure that they make time to offer consultations so that the best decision can be made. Being a devil's advocate empowers someone to speak up with concerns. Each role has a specific job description; when combined, they create an inclusive decision-making model.

There is also a very profound element to this practice at Mayo that gets its strength from Weis's Virtuous Circle of Trustworthy Leadership. Because of the permission and protection granted to decision-making participants by the ARCIVD approach, people are able to support the person who will be the devil's advocate or the person who has the ability to veto the project. They provide this support by living up to the values of the organization, sharing information with each other, and fulfilling their own responsibilities. It is a system that works when all participants cooperate, and it is a system that needed to be driven by a person with the position power of Weis.

As everyone who has ever been in a leadership role knows, comfort with your ability to move through uncertainty and risk does not guarantee a good night's sleep. You may be prepared and have confidence in your team's ability to go forward and make the right decisions, yet risk and uncertainty are always there. Since 2009, Weis's attention has been firmly directed at health care reform and all of the questions swirling around that. With a fair culture in place, and people's experience in being a devil's advocate and asking challenging questions, the negotiable elements of health care changes are on the table at Mayo, being addressed in thoughtful and intense discussions.

"The biggest challenge for us now is health care reform. My goal is to help us navigate it and stay Mayo Clinic in spite of it all. I don't think people fully understand what the impact could be on health care, particularly for Mayo Clinic," Weis says. "We really set the bar when it comes to quality health care. If we are all trying to operate on Medicare reimbursement, I don't think we can be Mayo Clinic and provide the same caliber of care. We will never give up our values or our focus on the patient, so something has to give. If you talk about what keeps me up at night, it's health care reform and that I'm unsure about what it will mean for us." As Weis and other leaders at Mayo surely know, risk never goes away; it just changes its shape and reappears in a new form.

There is much that is strategic in the plans and practices of people at Mayo. They would not be held in such high esteem if they weren't brilliant, creative, and innovative in what they do. Yet what truly sets them apart are their actions —like those of Shirley Weis— that rest on deeply held values that guide their work and support their movement through

I work as a supervisor in the outpatient desk operations area in the cancer center. To be successful, I first listened a lot. I went through the same training as my employees. I wanted to know what was going on, how they did things. I wrote down things I thought could change, heard them out as we went through, asked questions. I think anytime you go into a new role you need to build trust before you can make any change. That was advice given to me from a fellow manager, and it has worked out well for me.

—*Mayo Clinic supervisor*

the Virtuous Circle. It is this movement of leaders along the path of Trustworthy Leadership that provides the greatest opportunity to respond to the destabilizing effects of risk.

ROBERT W. BAIRD & CO.: UNCOVERING AND DEVELOPING KNOWLEDGE

We often gain a sense of security from our knowledge as we call on it to guide us through the many choices we need to make every day. Making a choice is often a relatively simple task that moves us quickly through the uncertainty we feel before the choice is made. *Do I want vanilla or chocolate? Should I wear a sweater or a jacket?* These daily choices happen so rapidly that often we don't even recognize that uncertainty was present, just for a moment, before we chose.

The knowledge that we carry with us helps us to make quick choices. Knowledge that we know how to access helps us with other decisions. And the knowledge that we know is out there, yet takes longer to find, helps us with choices that are more complex. The space before each of these types of choice is characterized by uncertainty. As the complexity of the decision grows, the uncertainty we face grows as well—as does our need for more creative and useful knowledge to guide our choices.

At work, knowing who to go to when you want an answer to your question makes life easier. Rather than hunting around for the information that might solve your dilemma, if you can go to the source and get things settled quickly, so much the better—then you can move on to the next task or decision that needs your attention. Most everyone inside an organization has a network of contacts—their sources—who ensure that questions are answered and projects are completed on time. But who are your sources for the questions that you don't know about, the projects that haven't even started yet, and the opportunities out there that haven't been identified?

Our ability to uncover, develop, and apply knowledge to the choices facing us in the unknown future is enhanced when we are well prepared to handle the risks associated with decision making. Anxiety that might interfere with clear thinking will be reduced, and the positive excitement that is generated when pursuing an opportunity will grow. It is here, at this crossover point, after Trustworthy Leaders have created systems to address risk that the importance of developing and applying knowledge is most keenly felt.

An internal knowledge bank, whether specifically identified as such or not, will serve as the repository of learnings from previous challenges and as the source of guidance for pursuing the opportunities ahead. Leaders who identify and develop sources of knowledge within their organization and then exploit them—in the best sense of the word—will have tapped a natural wellspring to serve as a sustainable source for future growth. This is exactly what has happened at Robert W. Baird & Co. within their Human Capital group. Lori Lorenz, managing director and Human Capital director, crafted Baird's approach to knowledge development, with strong support from CEO Paul Purcell and Chief Human Capital Officer Leslie Dixon. Her Trustworthy Leadership has influenced Baird's approach to knowledge development, and has fueled the company's approach to making the choices that are taking them from uncertainty to opportunity every day.

A unique part of what is happening at Baird is the degree to which the pursuit of organizational knowledge and the promotion of people's individual growth and learning are guided by the same philosophy. Lorenz and her team have created a unique approach to ensuring that the skills and abilities of a support person are developed within the same overarching framework as the skills and abilities of a leading investment analyst. The skills that each person will use in his or her job are distinct, as are the specific tactics used to help people develop and share their expertise. Yet what I found so distinctive about the approach at Baird is the degree to which development efforts are being consciously guided by an overarching commitment to everyone's value.

The development of every person, and every skill set, is linked through the deeply held belief that the organization is enhanced by every single person's contributions to Baird's repository of knowledge. This future-oriented strategy, being fully implemented through the work of the Human Capital group, is transforming the training, coaching, mentoring, and experiential learning programs at Baird. The goal is to develop knowledge for the next generation of financial service opportunities. And all of this is occurring within the current swirl of uncertainty facing the industry. With this approach, leaders at Baird anticipate being poised to take on opportunities far sooner than their competitors.

As Lorenz describes the distinction of what is happening at Baird, she's able to contrast her approach to what she sees in many other organizations, and to what used to exist at Baird. "Many people are still looking at human resource work as transactional, tactical work that is reactionary. Part of our purpose [in the Human Capital group] is to be more proactive, more strategic in our thinking, creating a partnership at the table. That was part of our goal in our transformation and merging of the two departments of Human Resources and Baird University. We wanted to create an all-encompassing talent management mind-set and be a better business partner at the table when thinking about the human capital needs and efforts that will build a better business for Baird going forward. That's what we're trying to embrace and have the organization embrace."

The merger that Lorenz talks about—between Human Resources and Baird University (where all training and development courses were offered)—brought together two different sets of activities that support knowledge development and talent management. As an example of what has changed over the past few years, Lorenz described the integration that has occurred among the many different components of the talent management process. "Historically we looked at each component as a one-off—here are our leadership development programs, here's our performance management effort, here's what we've done on the training and development side, here's how we pay people. We'd not thought about them from the broader, bigger picture of how we could integrate them so that they all tapped into the same source and fed back out to our future growth strategy.

"A good example is the leadership development piece. On that front, our ability to identify what we know have been successful traits of leaders at the firm should trickle into how we build our leadership development curriculum, how we build our career development offerings for those who aspire to be leaders one day, how we hold people accountable to those leadership traits from a performance management perspective, developing consistency in how we look at leaders and hold them accountable and then ultimately translating all of that into how we pay and reward people. That's one example, but if you think of the talent management lifecycle, every piece needs to be interwoven and strategically positioned so that one feeds the next."

Baird, like many companies, had relied on its more piecemeal approach for years. Yet, propelled by uncertainty in the marketplace and CEO Paul Purcell's deeply held belief in the value of everyone's contributions, Lorenz began to imagine that something could be different. Starting at the top of the organization, the strategic initiatives of the firm have been connected to overall development goals and also connected to the performance management process. Lorenz's commitment to consider the entire human capital landscape of the organization as a resource for future growth has propelled Baird to develop their knowledge resources from a unique, integrated perspective.

For this approach to work, Lorenz needed to be in an environment in which she could gather information from all the different delivery sources and have some creative free rein to propose new structures, new reporting relationships, and a cross-functional open platform for continued information sharing and development of new ideas. Luckily for her, and for Baird, open information sharing is part of Baird's DNA, and Lorenz is enjoying the success and challenge of the transformation process. "We are headed in the right direction and making really good progress. We moved much of the transactional HR work into a centralized area so that we have people dedicated to those services who make sure that our support doesn't slip there. We thus freed up a group of people within human capital to focus on the forward-looking strategy work and business partnering."

What Lorenz is able to do—think long term and focus on strategy—is absolutely essential to the creation of a knowledge-intensive firm that can move through uncertainty to pursue multiple opportunities. And she has the full backing of Purcell. According to Purcell, it is this ability to pursue a forward-looking long-term development strategy that is fueling the success of Baird. "One big issue with Americans is that we want everything right now. And we need to change the way that people think." Purcell is a big proponent of what he calls "the basic values" of working hard for the long term, setting long-term goals, and having leaders who look to the future, not next quarter. As he says, "The people who get us in trouble are the people who want too much too fast."

Purcell is very clear that a key reason for his success is that he delivers concrete results. "We generate good ROE, and I can pay people competitively. You've got to deliver results. There's no question about what we need to do. What we have complete power over is how we do it—that defines who we are. If we have a lot of body bags when we get there, nobody's happy. If we do it the right way, that's a different story. During the downturn, we wanted to keep the team together. Not because it's a feel-good, but the consistency of the team over the long term matters. I believe that fervently. The surest way we could do that was to give pay cuts to the top fifteen people at the firm. Everybody bought in. You walk out of that meeting, and you know you're going to win long term because we kept the team together. We'll protect the franchise and the people in the franchise. If you go into some of our competitors, they are cesspools of winners and losers."

Purcell's willingness to reduce the salaries of the top fifteen people at the firm to ensure the long-term stability of the team is a no-brainer on the surface. A short-term sacrifice was made by the leaders of the organization to support the greater good to be achieved in the future. He made a decision to ensure greater stability during a time of uncertainty that would enable the firm to better pursue opportunities in the future. Although Purcell's actions are only too rare in other firms, at Baird they are expected. And they are supportive of what Lorenz is trying to do across the firm with knowledge development.

Individuals can move out of uncertainty for themselves by actively choosing to develop their minds and engage in creative idea generation activities. This requires an environment of trust and support in which people's interest in exploring is encouraged by opportunities—both structured and unstructured—that feature openness, new ideas, and diverse opinions, with little in the way of judgment and constraints. This happens at Baird.

The combination of full support from the CEO and an ability to create a strategic, future-oriented human capital strategy is having its impact. Mark Kindler, in private wealth management, has been with Baird for eighteen years. He is clear that he can always count on people throughout Baird to help find solutions to internal challenges or to meet the needs of a client. "Here, everybody feels that if there is a way they can help to get a good end solution, they want to do that—you have the backup and the resources. It's like this is the largest small company you could work for. The capabilities here make it feel like there is nothing we can't do." Kindler is aware of the depth of knowledge available to him at Baird—and of the possibility to create more.

Laura Thurow, co-director of PWM Research, also benefited from the opportunities available to develop knowledge—her own, and Baird's. Thurow started at Baird in equity research, yet after five years she felt her interest waning. Rather than keep quiet and look outside the firm, she let people know that she was interested in something else. "I loved Baird and wanted to stick around, so I talked to people about what they did, and word traveled up to my manager's manager. He called me into his office one day and said, 'Hey, I heard you've been talking with people. Tell me what you want and what your plans and goals are.' We talked, and he asked if I'd be interested in looking at other opportunities if they came up."

Thurow responded positively, and within two weeks she was called back into his office with the offer of a new possibility. "He saw the potential to leverage my skill set of being an analyst with a different client base. For me, that was before I even knew what I wanted to do. He saw this link and opportunity and encouraged and helped me to pursue that, which I firmly believe is unique to this firm."

Thurow's story highlights the power of what Lorenz and Purcell talked about earlier in this chapter—taking the long-term view, keeping the team together, recognizing the knowledge inherent in each team member and pursuing knowledge development opportunities for the future benefit of the firm. It is a perfect combination of Purcell's vision and Lorenz and her team's ability to use that vision as part of the human capital strategy that leverages talent throughout the firm. Thurow—and her knowledge, contacts, and commitment to the firm—are all staying with Baird, and that is of great value to the organization.

In some firms, the "talking to people" that Thurow engaged in when she first realized that she wanted to try something different would be construed as disloyal to her team or group, and rather than being supported, it would be shut down. Such actions set off a cascade of consequences that severely limit future growth and development opportunities for the person involved and the organization. A person in Thurow's position who gets shut down can become risk-averse, which decreases her value to the firm. If her ability to contribute is tied solely to the team of which she is a member, then the whole organizational team loses out. Yet at Baird, Thurow was seen as a member of Baird as a whole, and at that time she was contributing in equity research. The entire approach to helping her move from the uncertainty of what could be next to the opportunity of contributing in another area is a micro-example of the larger effort being implemented at Baird.

Lorenz is clear that the implementation of the new human capital approach at Baird has a few more years to roll out and completely develop. And she always has her eye on the future opportunities that will come Baird's way. "It's an interesting journey that we're on, and I couldn't be more pleased, because I've felt that we've needed to connect the dots for a long time. I think it's the next step on our journey of leadership. I really believe that."

Knowledge is most valuable when it is a shared resource, which is how it is viewed at Baird. People who are constantly developing new skills will be able to use the knowledge currently available to them and contribute new insights to the collective pot for whatever comes next. The growing knowledge bank serves as a source of options for moving through uncertainty. Organizations and people can consider more permutations when knowledge is plentiful. Those organizations that are best at creating shared knowledge are creating a shared future for everyone. Less uncertainty and more opportunities—exactly what leadership is about.

> One of the things I am encouraged by is that I have seen the firm grow from a regional to a national firm. Management over the years has been able to constantly evaluate the strengths and weaknesses of the firm and grow the areas where opportunities have existed and that gave them more balance. In spite of a lot of disasters we have seen, we have been able to avoid a lot of those problems. We've survived and gained market share. They've been able to look out externally to see what the risks are. That's encouraging to me.
> —*Baird employee*

W. L. GORE & ASSOCIATES: APPLYING WISDOM

What is the advantage of being wise? We often identify people as wise when their actions enable them to live a fulfilling and enjoyable life. People who are wise are frequently asked for advice or commentary on how they have faced challenges, and they are often looked to as role models. At times an aura of mystery surrounds someone who is seen as wise, as the rest of us try to figure out what it is exactly that the wise person has achieved and how we could do so as well.

Organizations in which wisdom is present share some of the same characteristics as wise people—in part because wise people can be found inside of them, and also because collective wisdom is evident in how the organization has pursued success. Collective wisdom is more than the sum of each individual's wise thoughts and actions. In a practical sense, the collective wisdom inside an organization supports people's ability to make value-based or ethical judgments and follow through with actions that mirror those judgments. In a more profound sense, collective wisdom supports a group's ability to make significant decisions that entail forgoing a short-term benefit or opportunity for the realization of a deeper benefit.

I believe that collective wisdom is more readily created, shared, and applied in great workplaces where trust is present. One tremendous benefit of trust, which we experience most intensely in our closest relationships, is that when people trust each other, they are more willing to share. In an organization with Trustworthy Leaders, people are more willing to move forward together and share their wisdom within the group, based on the collective trust embedded in their relationships. As we move along the path from uncertainty to opportunity, there are no better companions than trust and shared wisdom.

W. L. Gore & Associates is a perfect company to use as an example of the ways in which wisdom can be applied to the benefit of the organization. Perfect not because it is flawless, but because of the high levels of self-awareness at Gore—in individuals, among people together in their teams, and throughout the organization as a whole. This self-awareness, combined with the foundational values of the organization, guides people's actions and supports the development and application of deep wisdom. The culture of Gore—and the wisdom that exists within it—enables the organization to move from uncertainty to opportunity all the time, with all of the normal imperfections of human and organizational life still present.

Gore is one of only five companies to have been included on every list of the 100 Best Companies to Work for in America since the inception of that list in 1984. They have achieved this distinction primarily due to the resonance and endurance of their culture. Gore's strength is visible to outsiders in its innovative products, creative idea generation, and financial success. The source of all this strength—the culture and the deep wisdom embedded in it—is a bit more elusive to describe, yet clearly experienced by all who work at Gore.

Bill Gore, one of the company's founders, often spoke of the importance of freedom and dreams when he talked about what would make his company successful. He wanted people to experience freedom in the workplace—which he characterized as a minimum of rules, regulations, and bureaucracy. If freedom was in place, then people would be able to pursue their dreams. And dreams are what would enable people to accomplish great things. This was Bill Gore's wisdom. It is a very simple equation that he followed and it enabled him to lead a good life. And he believed that freedom and dreams could help the organization to be successful—to live a good life as an organization—as well.

Yet how do you create and lead in an organization based on this kind of deep wisdom?

A number of practical steps were taken at Gore to help the company follow the wisdom of its founders. To support the idea of freedom, bureaucracy is at a minimum, and any visible evidence of hierarchy is squashed. People are on a first-name basis with each other, most work units are kept below two hundred so all unit members can know each other, and people are free to ask for help from whomever they think will be the best resource. These aspects of the structure of Gore's workplace are practical in the sense that they can be seen and experienced by people on a daily basis, not because they are practices in place in lots of other companies.

In Chapter Four, associates' ability to determine who they will choose to follow was documented as a tremendous strength of the organization. Practical wisdom is evident in this system as well—it works for the organization and has contributed greatly to the success of the business. Yet for people who are not familiar with Gore's culture or perhaps are afraid of the freedom inherent in this act of choice, seeing the practical wisdom in this step can be difficult. Their vision is blurred by the uniqueness of the activity. Yet it works for Gore, and this is one of the ways we can find evidence of wisdom—in a willingness to search for what works rather than follow a predefined path.

Rather than accepting uncertainty about whether a leader-follower relationship will be smooth, the practical wisdom applied at Gore ensures that followers are able to choose the people whom they want to follow, thus eliminating that uncertainty. This allows people to move forward together and tackle opportunities that might otherwise be missed due to inefficiencies created by weak relationships. Where did the wisdom for this arrangement come from? Initially, from the mind of Bill Gore—then as people tried it and it worked, it spread to collective success throughout the organization. Applied wisdom helped people move away from the uncertainty of leader-follower relationships to the opportunity provided by strong teams of smart, competent people working well together.

Let's go back to Bill Gore's wisdom. He wanted people to experience freedom so that they could pursue their dreams. He believed that great things would be accomplished if people had great expectations, and that the way to nurture that is to dream. He believed that when people think small they get bogged down in details; he wanted people to think big. To support this, he and others designed a number of structural elements and practices for the company that would lead them to their profound goal. Michael Pacanowsky, a longtime Gore associate, said, "Without being arrogant, Bill was very confident in what he brought to the enterprise, as were others. They believed that if the dream captivated them, they could figure out a way to make it happen."

These beliefs are all a part of Bill Gore's legacy to the company that bears his name. That company is very different now from the way it was during those early years. There are nine thousand associates around the world in thirty countries, and a variety of products being used in many industries that didn't exist when the company was founded. The uncertainty-opportunity continuum faced by Gore's leaders and associates is similar to the one faced earlier, but it has been magnified tremendously. There are many more opportunities available to consider, there is much more uncertainty in the marketplace, and there is a greater need for deep wisdom to guide the organization forward. So how do the leaders at Gore continue to develop and pass on wisdom in such a way that freedom and dreams can continue to flourish?

One way this happens at Gore is through the process of asking people to make commitments. Just as associates are asked to choose who they want to follow, they are also asked to choose their projects. The choice of a project to work on is part of the process of having the freedom to dream. Underlying wisdom guides the action and moves an associate, in this first act, from the uncertainty of not knowing what he or she is going to work on to the freedom of choice and the experience of making a commitment. The opportunity on the other side is the dream that emerges from the choices the associate makes.

Jacques Rene, an associate whose current commitment is to lead and support the Bioprocess Solutions team in the Industrial Products Division, has been with Gore for nearly fourteen years. He remembers that when he was first hired at Gore he was told, "We don't know what to do with you. But we think you're a talented guy and here's a core commitment that will be a good start for you. Then we'll just let it fly." In some ways "just let it fly" can be interpreted as code for "We're going to dream for a bit." This could be an uncertain position to be in as a new employee in any organization, yet, given that Gore's underlying cultural wisdom supported the decision to "let it fly," Rene found himself in an environment that offered the freedom he needed to join in the process of dreaming.

Rene has certainly been successful at Gore, given the length of his career and the varied commitments he has been able to make. Yet when he talks about his time at Gore, it is not the upward mobility that he focuses on, but the inward mobility, the opportunities he has had to learn and grow. "Things just develop naturally over time," he said. One of the first commitments Rene made was as a product specialist for one of the hot products of the late 1990s—fiber optic ribbon cable. Back then fiber optics technology was growing like crazy, yet the work team's initial experiments with the product didn't turn out as he'd wanted. "We did some testing on our product, and the results were not what we hoped for—there wasn't the differentiation in the telecommunications segment that we thought was going to be there. I had this news I had to share at a team meeting, and at the end of the day, my assumption was that the leaders in the room were going to make a decision in terms of what was going to happen with this."

After Rene shared the data and his analysis, to his surprise, he was also asked to propose the next move with this product initiative. "I never would have thought that the decision would be at my feet. I thought it would be folks in leadership who would have to make the call. Yet they said, 'No, you have the most knowledge in this. You did all the work and the testing. We want you to make the call in terms of the best course.'" And so it went; Rene was able to make the decision. He describes the experience as a firsthand taste of one of the company's core principles in action. That principle—"waterline"—asks that the person or people with the most knowledge relative to the decision being considered be the ones who are all involved in making the choice. "I thought, *Wow, waterline is really waterline.* The decision wouldn't sink the ship [go below the waterline], and the knowledge rests in the folks who are doing the work."

What happened for Rene in that meeting, and what he has been able to carry with him all these years, is a combination of freedom and dreams that have been turned into wisdom. He experienced both the freedom and commitment principles with his choice to join the fiber optics ribbon cable product initiative. He and his fellow associates were given the opportunity to envision what might be possible with the product, and they tested various scenarios for how their ideas could be realized in the business environment. What they envisioned didn't pan out as a product that could go to market with the differentiation they believed necessary for success. Their decision to not go forward reflected the waterline principle.

The wisdom that Rene carries with him from this experience is deeply held. He was able to connect the guiding wisdom provided by a founder who is no longer there with an invigorating experience in which the value of that wisdom was made real to him—through his *own* use of the wisdom. This is a striking example of how things are different at Gore. Along with living out the principles, people seek to enact the wisdom that first led to the creation of the principles. While considering this story, we should not overlook the fact that Rene and the fiber optics product team moved through the uncertainty of their situation with grace and confidence. The opportunity that they thought might be at the other end of their efforts didn't materialize, yet that didn't stop the process of living the principles and looking for the next opportunity.

Another associate who has benefited from the "freedom and dreams" wisdom at Gore is Mary Tilley, whose current commitment is as the global leader for human resource activities at Gore. Tilley came into Gore as a chemical engineer. Her first commitment was in product development in a manufacturing engineering group. "I then moved into the more customer-facing role of product specialist, yet I decided that what I really liked and gravitated toward were the teams and the people. At that time, there was a widely held belief that product specialists should not be sponsors so that they could remain focused on the success of the product. Yet I was always drawn into the people things, and we are always encouraged to pay attention to our skills and passions."

So, despite the general proscription against product specialists sponsoring people, Tilley ended up sponsoring lots of people. Her growth at work included moving into an engineering leadership role and then into the plant environment. She often found herself thinking of ways she could contribute, and she began to focus on creating broader development opportunities for engineers. "I realized all the work we were doing as engineers was in the context of something operational. So I started to focus on corporate initiatives around operational excellence and how we could improve our whole operations."

As Tilley tells the story of her career trajectory, her application of the underlying wisdom of life at Gore becomes visible. Tilley remembers always being encouraged to follow her skills and passions—something that many people at Gore talk about. In following her passions, she has experienced many of the qualities of Trustworthy Leadership. She has been included in discussions and opportunities, been given the freedom to choose to follow other people and create her own path, had open access to the information she needed, and been supported in her development. The wisdom of Gore that developed before her time has supported her movement through any number of uncertainties to continue to take on new opportunities.

Tilley now plays a major part in the recruitment and development of leaders at Gore and is able to apply the wisdom she developed to guide her own actions and support the work of the human resources team. "[I]f we think about our leaders having to understand and lead in this culture, there are two major things we look for," she said. "One is that they are collaborative by nature. We are a very collaborative company; we are not authoritarian or dictatorial. The second one is very easy to spot. We look for people who are okay with not having titles, who are not very focused on position or having the authority to say or do things." These are not attributes usually associated with people in leadership positions, yet they are completely appropriate to the culture at Gore. They reflect the underlying wisdom that freedom and dreams will help the organization to be successful.

When new leaders move into their positions at Gore, they are not generally expected to lead right away. Although some might assume this is part of a professional development strategy that gives a new leader time to get acclimated, at Gore the development of a leader's ability to lead is part of a longer-term strategy. Tilley explains, "As we hire people, we make sure it's pretty clear to them that although the intent may be that they lead something big, especially the broader leaders, they will probably come in and work in a hands-on capacity at first. There's a reason for that. People need to learn the business; other people need to get to know them. The culture is the biggest thing. Certainly, they come in with credibility in business or operations or whatever the technical part of their job may be. But we actually take a bit of time for them to work with the teams, so that we can see how it works before we move them or allow them to take on a broader leadership role." Another area in which the collective wisdom inside Gore is applied to a very practical task—developing leaders.

The leadership path at Gore starts with hands-on work, giving that person time to get to know people and gain credibility. But it's not credibility in terms of skills—it's credibility in terms of being able to work with the teams, be collaborative, and get used to the fact that as a leader, you won't have a title and you won't have the authority to order people to do certain things. Again, amazing wisdom in action—as Tilley says, the culture is the biggest thing at Gore. So the system has been set up to enable potential new leaders to experience the deep wisdom embedded in the culture before they are asked to apply the more practical wisdom contained in their skills.

Trustworthy Leaders who live within their Virtuous Circle that begins with honor are continuously developing and applying their wisdom. Wisdom will enable you to see the inherent risks of organizational life and to approach those risks with grace. Wisdom will support your efforts to seek out knowledge and find ways of developing and sharing new knowledge with others. And wisdom will enable you to move through the questions that inevitably arise as groups of people work together to create, produce, and deliver products and services in your organization. Wisdom is both practical and profound. It serves as the resting place and launch pad for the great ideas that fuel the success of great workplaces.

Often stories about W. L. Gore end with some proviso along the lines of "Don't try this experiment at home." People outside the company are often quite challenged by the descriptions of Gore's workplace practices—no hierarchy, no titles, people make their own commitments and choices. Although these practices may not be for everyone, what *is* for everyone is the way in which people at

> Although making money is a primary goal and is why we're in existence, it's really the other things we do as an enterprise that are the most important. Not only in terms of how we treat people, but in terms of how we deal with each other. Particularly in this day and age, where so many things you hear about Wall Street run amok have taken center stage, here at Gore we're all about the long term and what's right to do for the ongoing sustainability of the enterprise, instead of just short-term goals. That's one thing I'm particularly proud of.
>
> —W. L. Gore associate

Gore connect to the deeply held wisdom of the organization. This wisdom is not the rocket science involved in the design and development of their most successful products; rather, it is the human science that everyone can tap into. This human science consists of a few key principles that people at Gore have named freedom, fairness, commitment, and waterline. They are principles that you can adapt and use as a Trustworthy Leader in your own organization.

CONTINUING THE CIRCLE

We cannot control the world around us, yet we can prepare for how to best respond. Developing your understanding of uncertainty, strategies and skills for moving through it, and an appreciation for its place in organization management are key tasks of successful leadership. There is no doubt that too much uncertainty—the feeling that there are "too many balls in the air"—is uncomfortable and makes taking action and moving forward difficult. Yet for most leaders, dealing with uncertainty—ideally, with grace and integrity—is part of the job. So what would it take to get you to move forward through uncertainty with as much grace as the people we've just read about? For myself, it often comes down to wanting to be on the other side of whatever I'm facing so that I *can* keep going forward.

A recent opinion piece in the *Wall Street Journal* titled "How Uncertainty Cripples Us" quoted studies showing that, as the level of uncertainty about the outcome of a decision increases, our ability to effectively consider all of our options diminishes.[1] Researchers found that at precisely the time when you could benefit from considering a variety of options, the destabilizing effect of uncertainty causes you to *limit* your choices.

Given that uncertainty itself is inherently destabilizing, what should you do to counter this effect? I recommend that you do what the great leaders profiled in this chapter and throughout this book have done: build trust-based relationships with colleagues. Trust is a stabilizing force in our lives. When you present yourself as trustworthy, you diminish the negative effects of uncertainty. By being trustworthy, you help people open their minds and share their ideas. This flow of ideas will provide you with many options to tackle whatever challenge you are facing, increasing the variety of choices and actions you can take and giving you and your organization a tremendous advantage in ensuring the success of your efforts.

Put simply: uncertainty turns into opportunity when mediated by trustworthy behavior.

In the next and final chapter, I will share with you a few more stories that richly illustrate how great Trustworthy Leaders call on all of the elements of the Virtuous Circle to help them lead their organizations. These examples affirm the tremendous benefits that come to people and organizations when trust is present.

The Roots of Pursuing Opportunities

Lori Lorenz has an idea for what she'd like to see in the world, and she's using it to help guide her actions as Baird's Human Capital director. Her vision is one that many of us probably share—a world in which people are respected and able to develop their talents, enjoy their personal lives, and be healthy. It's a pretty tall order, yet that hasn't stopped Lorenz from keeping her vision ever present as she moves forward at Baird.

Where did all of this come from? Lorenz gives a great deal of credit to her mentors at Baird. "If you had asked me sixteen years ago where I'd be, I'm not quite sure I would say that I would be right here. When you come into Baird, you don't necessarily have a defined career path in front of you. This organization is really good at helping you navigate and figure that out while you're here." Lorenz is a big believer in capitalizing on people's strengths and talents—trying to shape and mold positions and operating practices based on people's skills and expertise. She herself was not forced onto a predetermined path at Baird, and now other people at Baird benefit from the freedom that she first experienced there.

It's a model that has worked very well for Baird. "We believe we get more capability [and] more skill and tap more of a person's potential by handling it in that manner than some prescribed manner of a detailed path. For me, my career just sort of started to grow over the years. My responsibilities grew, and my expertise developed in lots of different areas because I was afforded the opportunity to explore."

Lorenz's relationship with Leslie Dixon (chief Human Capital officer), her supervisor and mentor, has had a deep and lasting impact on her approach to her work. "Leslie hired me and became my mentor along the way. I always felt that Leslie treated me as a partner, not as a subordinate, and that we were always working toward the same goals. We could leverage one another's skills, capabilities, and expertise." Lorenz knows that the mentoring relationship she benefited from has been key to her success, and she actively encourages others to find mentors for themselves. And because of the freedom she's had to imagine a better future for the organization, everyone is benefiting from the changes being made.

"For a number of years I had been feeling like we needed a new model for how we were tapping into all the strengths and talents of our people, and it didn't come soon enough for me! We've put so much energy in the last year into making this transformation happen, bringing together Baird University and Human Resources. I am at the point now where the reality of the transformation is hitting me. It's not necessarily a struggle, but it is a challenge."

Lorenz is letting go of some things, shifting responsibilities and letting her business partners and the experts on her team take over. "Change is difficult," she acknowledges. "We tend to hang on to what's most comfortable, and it is a little scary to let go of that, but I know it's the right answer, to do that and turn my attention to the broader human capital issues in the firm. We have a very strong culture, a very rich culture. It's the foundation of who we are. We have many, many best practices in place, and we can always improve."

CHAPTER EIGHT

HOW IT ALL COMES TOGETHER

Have you ever had an experience during which the pieces of the puzzle fit together more smoothly, or with less effort than previously? You've been working hard on a project with your colleagues, trying to meet deadlines, resolve dilemmas, and find answers to puzzling questions. At a certain point things start to click; the struggle falls away, the questions diminish, and you go forward, moving in the right direction, making choices, confident that in the end you will arrive at your goal.

You share information with others and they reciprocate. The professional development session your colleague went to a few months ago pays off with new insights she's able to provide to the whole group. You find your voice, saying what's needed and appropriate, and acting in ways that reflect your deeply held values. The team's efforts converge, you all find the answers you seek, and the challenge of the situation recedes behind you.

I believe we are able to create and participate in these situations because of our trustworthy behavior and the relationships that are formed based in trust. When we act with integrity, being faithful to the values and beliefs that create our Virtuous Circle of Trustworthy

Leadership, we gain tremendous rewards—cooperation, creativity, and the successful resolution of dilemmas among them.

A recent experience of mine gave me an excellent opportunity to use the framework of the Virtuous Circle to look for insights into the power of trust and trustworthy behavior. My experience reinforced for me the special and unique nature of relationships based in trust and strengthened my confidence that I could call on that trust to see me through whatever challenge I might face in the future. Periodically reviewing events in our lives—times when we've struggled and times when we've had great success—is very important for keeping the lessons of trustworthy behavior ever present.

My experience was an enjoyable one that became challenging as circumstances changed, providing a valuable metaphor for many of the situations we face as leaders in organizations. I like to go hiking and, luckily for me, my wonderful friend Marc does too. On one occasion we were in southern France, hiking along a beautiful yet narrow trail in the mountains. We started our hike late on a winter day, and darkness set in before we were finished. My night vision is pretty awful, yet Marc's is excellent, so I was content to follow his lead. There was minimal moonlight from the sky, and it became even darker as we continued, until both of us were stumbling over branches and rocks.

We arrived at a junction where we were completely unsure of the trail. It could have been straight ahead, yet it also appeared there was a trail off to the side, down the hill. We had a cell phone to call for help if we needed it, yet we didn't know exactly where we were, so we couldn't really ask someone to find us—and we were determined to figure this out. The light from the cell phone was weak, and Marc, not wanting to damage his night vision, had used it minimally for guidance. He decided to go down the hill to see whether the side trail really was passable, while I stayed put. I realized that I had my camera with me and it had a flash. I let Marc know I was going to use the flash to see what was around us, figuring that my poor night vision would be worse after the flash, yet maybe I'd be able to see a trail in the bright light.

Marc stayed away so his sight wouldn't be dimmed, and bingo, the flash illuminated the trail ahead of me—covered over by branches from the tall trees around us, yet clearly visible in that flash of light.

I called to Marc, he came back up the hill, and we proceeded on our way. The flash had really knocked out my night vision, so I not only followed Marc but was completely dependent on him for the next few minutes. After a while, we came to the end of the trail and the road out to where our car was parked. The night sky was beautiful, and there was even a small waterfall cascading down the side of the mountain where the trail ended. It was stunning, we were safe, and we'd had a wonderful adventure.

This story provides a great picture of the joys of night hiking, and also describes a powerful experience of trust. Marc and I were experienced hikers, just as business leaders are experienced at running their enterprises. We had made plans to go hiking in a certain area—a place where others had hiked but we'd never been to before. In the same way that you might decide to make a certain product or provide a service that was new to your organization, we set out believing that our previous experience would help us successfully complete the hike.

We were prepared with the right resources: appropriate clothing and boots, water, food, a phone, and a camera. From an organizational perspective, all of the basics were in place—training and development, resources, and skills. Yet all the basics don't necessarily prepare you for uncertainty, and that's what we faced as it became late and the sky darkened. As we saw in the previous chapter, in any situation, no matter how well prepared you are, there will be times when a new variable demands that you change your plans. And this is where the Virtuous Circle proves its worth.

Marc and I trusted each other completely and were able to work through the uncertainties we faced as we searched for the end of the trail. Although neither of us had previously given much thought to feeling honored to be the friend of the other, this element came into play just as it does for a Trustworthy Leader in the workplace. We each felt that we were neither better nor worse than the other and that our relationship was reciprocal; we were aware both of our position power and the strength of our personal relationship.

We also were inclusive in our behavior toward each other. We all show our trustworthiness by letting others know that we believe in their value, are interested in their ideas, and are willing to fairly share the benefits that come to us. We do this as Trustworthy Leaders in a variety of situations, even on the hiking trail. Marc and I knew we were valuable to each other, exchanged ideas often as we decided which way to go, and shared the benefits of what we learned.

Although hypothetically it is possible that once I'd identified the trail ahead of us, Marc could have come back up and taken off on his own down the trail, there would have been little benefit and significant cost. I was inclusive with Marc and shared my discovery with him because I trusted that we would share the benefits of this knowledge. And he reciprocated, continuing to share his skills as a leader as we moved forward on the trail. We included each other in our actions without any second-guessing—inclusion is a natural part of trustworthy behavior and trust-based relationships.

For most of the hike, Marc and I switched off between leading and following. When hiking in daylight on a marked trail, we were both able to serve in both capacities. Yet when darkness came, I needed to follow. And Marc, knowing that I was unable to see well as the darkness increased, did a great job of engaging me as we continued to hike. One of the beauties of trust-based relationships is that we bring others with us as we move forward, and because of trust, people are willing to follow. It was easy for me to choose to follow Marc, confident that I would continue to be treated respectfully. We accompanied each other to the end of the hike, and certainly this experience contributed to our strong bond of trust.

In a less respectful situation I might also have followed, yet would have done so out of fear of being left on the trail—a form of compliance behavior. Following Marc out of fear might have gotten me to the end of the trail, yet the hike would have been much less enjoyable and, once over, I would have been more inclined to forget the whole thing rather than add it to the pot of great experiences to learn from and tell others about. I also would have been less trusting that I could rely on Marc for help in the future.

During the hike and when we needed to make choices, Marc and I shared information with each other in ways we could understand, allowing both of us to participate in decisions. When we finished our hike, we had a great laugh, talking over what we had seen and experienced—the lessons learned (maybe next time we'd bring a flashlight) and the surprising beauty of the unexpected waterfall at the end of the trail.

In organizations, these types of thoughtful and productive review discussions—about what worked and what didn't, and what could be improved in the future—happen when trust is present. These discussions enable teams to develop the skills they need to move through projects more smoothly the next time, and to prepare themselves for the next wave of uncertainty that they'll surely face. When leaders create positive, inclusive environments that promote trustworthy behavior, all participants know that they are valuable and invited to contribute. People can share their input and take lessons from the discussion to use for the next task.

My story illustrates for me—and, I hope, for you—how each element of the Virtuous Circle contributed to Marc's and my ability to get out of a difficult situation. Yet when it was happening I wasn't thinking of honor or inclusion or followership. I was simply acting and responding, making choices in the context of a trustworthy relationship. Trust is what guided us.

In this final chapter, I share three stories that illustrate Trustworthy Leadership in action—stories that illustrate the powerful environment that is created when trust is developed and its benefits are shared. These stories bring to life the underlying elements of the complete Virtuous Circle and illustrate how each leader's lifetime of experiences helps him or her to act with integrity and engage in trustworthy behavior. The stories also document the many benefits that come to each leader, his or her colleagues, and the organization as a whole.

As you read through these stories, ask yourself how you would have approached a similar situation, and how you would have called on the elements of your Virtuous Circle to guide you. There is no perfect approach to moving through the uncertainty that you are sure to face as a leader, yet reflecting on your experiences and the experiences of others can help you to be well prepared.

THINGS WILL BE DIFFERENT . . .

I first introduced Hoar Construction in Chapter Five, to show how their information-sharing practices support people's active participation in the life of the organization. Rob Burton, the current CEO, has described his position there as a dream come true, something he began preparing for when he was just thirteen and worked at Hoar during the summer, doing odd jobs to develop his carpentry and building skills. His career trajectory at Hoar included stints as an assistant superintendent and job clerk and work in accounting, marketing, and finally project management, where he served as a vice president. He has been president and CEO of Hoar since 1996, seeing it grow from a $40 million company in the mid-1970s to close to a billion dollars in work and project management revenue in 2009.

Construction is known as a tough industry. Everything is driven by deadlines and negotiations—among contractors, subcontractors, city planners, architects, lawyers, and bankers—and there are significant risks in the building process itself. It's not an industry in which you immediately expect to find great workplaces characterized by high levels of trust. Stereotypes about trust being a "soft" quality can keep some people in "tough" industries from developing the skills needed to be trustworthy. Yet at Hoar, Trustworthy Leaders are what make the place so successful.

Burton is clear that Hoar has made a lot of changes over the years to become a great workplace. He watched five presidents lead the company before him, and he learned a lot from being on the receiving end of their behavior, which was sometimes effective, other times not. As a frontline employee and middle manager, he had many opportunities to consider how he might do things differently if given the chance. "I can remember thinking, *I know what it's like to be an employee in the company. I've done all those jobs and been treated in different ways by different people. I know what works and what doesn't.* I always had it in my mind that if I ever got to that position, it would be different." So in 1996, when he did "get to that position," he got his opportunity to try something different.

Early on, Burton emphasized the importance of creating a safe work environment, supporting the implementation of training programs for all employees. He was initially surprised by the impact that his personal support had on others' participation and willingness to contribute. "The greatest business lesson I've learned about what it means to be a CEO is that you get what you inspect, not what you expect." he said. "When I set out to create a safe working environment, I wanted to really improve our safety culture here. I began inspecting safety over and over again, talking about it, preaching about it. Everybody caught on and realized that this was important. What CEOs don't know is that they're constantly being watched; for good or for bad, they are in the spotlight. A lot of them don't want to admit it, and a lot of them will say it's unfair, but wherever they go, whatever they do, they are being watched. If you're not supervising something and you're not participating in it, then it is not going to work. My father taught me that. His saying was, 'You don't get what you expect, you get what you inspect, as long as you do it with respect.'"

This vignette is a wonderful example of the formative life lessons that people call on as their leadership skills grow and develop. For Burton, his father's words form a foundation for creating a safer work environment at Hoar. He actively participates in the implementation of safety programs, his role as CEO puts him in the spotlight, and his modeling of concern and interest influence the success of the program.

His position awareness affirms his sense of the honor inherent in the leadership role. Linking his father's wisdom to his own actions shows his awareness of the influence that significant personal relationships can have on our behavior. He reinforces this at Hoar by creating strong connections between senior and junior employees—important for both inclusion and followership. And to ensure the success of the safety program, Burton fosters both information sharing and people development. This is all evidence of movement through his Virtuous Circle.

There are many vignettes about Burton's growth as a Trustworthy Leader that could be told; of these, one that clearly illustrates his trustworthy actions concerns the codification of the company's core values. As Burton tells it, a significant change for the company came about in 2002 when he wanted to build consensus around the core values that would guide the firm's activities into the future. He had read the book *Good to Great* and liked it a lot; he wanted all of the company's officers to read it.

"We had a consultant come in and guide us through the process of determining our core values. That was one of the most fun weekends I ever spent," Burton said. "We all debated openly and honestly and argued about what our core values were. We actually had settled on three. We were almost through for the weekend, yet we knew there was something missing. We had settled on the golden rule, family-oriented, and stewardship. We thought that with those you could handle everything. Yet I kept saying, 'No, there's something missing.'"

Burton and the group of officers stepped away from their task, which was a wise move. It gave them all a chance to reflect on the core values they had affirmed and also to think about what was missing, what else was needed. "We went away from that weekend, yet kept thinking about it. Finally, I reached back into what I had learned over all my years from those other people that I'd worked for, and it came to me. It was the relentless pursuit of improvement. Those men taught me that there's always a better way to do things, and that you can never rest on your laurels. You always have to be looking ahead, and you always have to improve." That was a key moment in Burton's ability to have an impact as a Trustworthy Leader.

Hoar Construction Core Values

Golden Rule—It is our desire that all Hoar employees strive to be exemplary in their treatment of others. Honesty and integrity will be foremost in our every thought and decision. Fairness, caring, and mutual respect will be evident in our every action.

Family Oriented—We must have a sincere respect for our families. Compassion and understanding will define our character as we consider the needs of others.

Relentless Pursuit of Improvement—With a disciplined and determined work ethic, we must strive for improvement in our company, our community, and ourselves. Our recruiting and training programs will be unsurpassed in leading people to succeed.

Stewardship—We are entrusted with the resources of others and the future of this company. As caretakers we will add value to each other, our clients, our projects, and our community.

Burton's willingness to struggle, along with the executive team, to identify the final or "missing" significant value that guided the leadership practices at Hoar is not earth-shattering, yet it is illuminating. He trusted that taking additional time and thinking deeply about what was important to him and the organization would help clarify what he was looking for.

Burton wasn't the only one who found the experience of that long weekend to be triumphant and significant. Douglas Eckert, executive vice president for Business Operations, spoke of what he learned while going through the process of codifying the company's core values.

"I'd say the difference in the values process that I saw here was that it was reflective of what people already believed. I've watched lots of companies post goals as values, but their leaders don't necessarily point the company in all phases toward those values. Here, the difference really was that I watched a group of people sit in a room and very intently—skeptically at first, but intently—say, 'Well, what is it that we like about working with each other? What don't we like about working with each other?' The conclusion was three out of four of our core values that we have now. What separated this 'values' process from others was that the values [we identified] are reflective of what we already believe and think [as a company], not what we'd like to be."

Employees at Hoar also talk about the impact that those core values have had on their work. During focus group discussions, when asked what makes them proud to work for Hoar Construction, people often cited the core values and the connection between the company's values and their own as a source of great strength. Mark Hendricks, a contract manager, said he works at Hoar because the company's core values match his own: "We're all cut from the same cloth, and it makes me proud to know that the company I work for holds the same values that I do personally."

Trippe Gray, a project manager, spoke about how the values of the company help everyone to reach higher: "What we're all striving for here every day is bigger than building buildings. That's where the core values and the envisioned future come in—we're all working to accomplish something that is bigger than just construction. The upper management in every division I've worked in, whether Houston or Tuscaloosa or Birmingham, practices the same core values that attracted me to this company in the first place."

And finally, Frank Marsac, a general superintendent, spoke of the motivation he feels from working at a company that has a strong, clear set of core values that are actually lived out: "A few years back, when they came up with the shared vision and core values, everybody said 'This is really what it's about.' This is what you get up every morning for. It's not 'I gotta put food on the table and I've got a hundred mouths to feed at home.' You want to feel good about what you do. It makes me feel good about coming to work here, that it's about a greater good."

Strong words—and powerful testimony to the impact that a shared sense of purpose and shared values can have on people's commitment to each other, to their work, and to the overall purpose of the company. These kinds of positive testimonials can inspire many people to try to follow a similar path. Yet they can also attract scorn and skepticism from people who haven't seen the development and implementation of a set of corporate values work successfully. Too often words can go up on the wall, yet people fail to live them out through their actions.

Rob Burton is very astute when it comes to the role that the CEO needs to play in ensuring the success of an effort like this. "The advice I would give to any CEO trying to follow or establish a great place to work is that you have to be committed yourself. You have to have a conversation with yourself and decide if you are really interested in this and if you really want it." That conversation you have with yourself is another way of saying that you need to be clear, to develop your Virtuous Circle, so that you can be effective as a Trustworthy Leader.

One of the questions that Burton is asked most frequently by people who wish that the leaders in their organizations would have that "conversation with yourself" concerns the potential financial impact of spending time developing and/or codifying a set of corporate values that will then be used to guide the business. Some people assume that the costs associated with taking time away from other work represent an unacceptable allocation of scarce financial and people resources. At Hoar Construction, the time spent on codifying the company's values and pursuing the creation of a great workplace is seen as time well spent.

"Lots of people want to know if there is a financial return on being a great place to work, and I want to say emphatically that we didn't care." Burton says they are doing this at Hoar because they *wanted* to work according to their core values. "We even decided that if it cost us money, it was the right thing to do—no matter what. We state at the beginning of our core values—and it's on everybody's screen saver here—that we will not stray from our core values for financial expediency or financial gain. They come first. Having done that, though, I will say that ever since 2002, when we instituted those core values and set a goal of being a great place to work, there has been nothing but growth and financial gain. I think there is a correlation there. There's just no question in my mind that happy employees do better work. When employees do better work, you get better results. The owners see it—they notice a difference in our company when they compare it to other companies."

Douglas Eckert sees it too, and he puts his assessment of the effort involved in codifying the core values into the broader context of the company's culture. "The culture is the key to the kingdom. If you want to be crass about it and talk about money, people can ask, "Is there a return on investment? Are you going to make more money because of it?" The answer is that I don't know if you can tie that together scientifically, but I'm 100 percent convinced that the company ultimately does better because we hire better people." Eckert is clear that if you work in an environment where every day that you come to work you're happy about being there and you enjoy the people around you, then you'll work harder and better.

As a specific example of one area in which Eckert believes that the investments made at Hoar have been beneficial, he cites the nature of the construction industry and how Burton's stance as a Trustworthy Leader has paid off. "Construction can be a litigious environment because there's so much going on, so much that can go wrong. We've been in the business sixty-nine years and our CEO has been in it over thirty. He's never been to court, and he's never been deposed. I defy you to find anyone in this industry that is as big as we are that has ever had that happen. It's because we tackle issues early on, we resolve them, and we focus so much on giving the person the benefit of the doubt and every opportunity to be heard. It's our culture. The culture is the core values and the treatment of the people."

Interestingly, the one person who went through the experience of identifying and codifying the core values who was surprised by the process and the outcome was the consultant who facilitated the weekend. As Burton relates it, the consultant kept saying how amazed he was by their process, that there was something strange about what was happening. Burton asked him what was wrong, and the consultant shook his head and said, "Nobody's mentioned money. No one has ever mentioned profit." Burton thought that was pretty funny. All the officers who were at the meeting agreed that the money would take care of itself. If people work well together and are skilled and smart about their approach, then profit should take care of itself—and that's exactly what's been happening at Hoar.

So what is it about Rob Burton that enabled his development as a Trustworthy Leader? Surely there is much that is personal to Burton that influenced his choices, yet what is personal is not exclusive—and this is one of the most important points to be made by his story. His experience of being influenced by the wisdom of his father, choosing a career in an industry that always fascinated him, learning from master craftsmen and exploring others' ideas, all point to values-based experiences that define what is important to him.

From his father's wisdom he develops a sense of honor and understands the power of relationships. Working in an industry he loves taps into a natural human desire to take pride in one's efforts, which can promote an interest in helping others find the same spark—not necessarily leading into the construction trades, but into an area of work that is fascinating for them. Learning from master craftsmen and exploring ideas point to the value of sharing information and developing others. All of these are building blocks for the creation of a Virtuous Circle that supports Trustworthy Leadership.

There is also, within Burton, a commitment to living a life in which his own values are consistent with those of his workplace. And he is one of the fortunate people who, because of his hard work and accomplishments, has had the opportunity to successfully pursue his commitment. People who work at Hoar Construction and their customers, suppliers, and community members are all the beneficiaries.

DAY-TO-DAY CONSISTENCY

At Recreational Equipment Incorporated, better known as REI, the idea of leading and working according to one's values was built into the original ethos of the company. Founded in 1938 by Lloyd and Mary Anderson, REI was established as an outdoor gear and apparel co-op.

Twenty-three mountaineers joined the Andersons to create a cooperative business. Lloyd Anderson felt strongly that people shouldn't make money off their friends, so the cooperative sharing of risks and rewards existed from the start.

Mary Anderson, who celebrated her one-hundredth birthday in 2009, continues to inspire people at REI. In 2009, the REI Foundation established the Mary Anderson Legacy Grant program in honor of her birthday and her contributions to REI throughout its rich history. The grant program supports nonprofits focused on helping young people be involved in the outdoors through hands-on nature exploration.

An Anderson Award, given annually to employees who embody the core values of REI, reflects Lloyd and Mary's original intentions for the co-op. It is a peer-based award given to employees whose accomplishments exemplify REI's core values and strategic plans, thus continuing the link between the values of the company and their business practices.

So what are REI's values? They are a concisely articulated series of statements—similar in many ways to those of Hoar—that provide guidance and a launching pad for action.

Authenticity
We are true to the outdoors.

Quality
We provide trustworthy products and services.

Service
We serve others with expertise and enthusiasm.

Respect
We listen and learn from each other.

Integrity
We live by a code of rock-solid ethics, honesty, and decency.

Balance
We encourage each other to enjoy all aspects of life.

The words contained in the values are not much different from those found in the value statements of any organization. So what makes it different at REI? The same thing that could be said about every organization profiled in this book—people at REI actively seek to live out their values. REI's leaders know that their specific efforts to be trustworthy are key to the culture and success of the enterprise. In some ways there is a collective Virtuous Circle at REI that is reinforced by leaders' behaviors. Everyone is invited in, yet the actions and words of the leaders start the process.

During my visit to REI, one of the programs I learned about that reflects people's deep commitment to living the values at REI is Base Camp. This program, essentially an employee orientation and welcoming program, is the place where all new employees learn about the core values of the company. The Base Camp program was refreshed in 2009 to include even more time focused on the core values, what they mean, why they were codified, and how people can use them to make decisions.

Erin Hass, first introduced in Chapter Two, was significantly involved in the reinvigoration of Base Camp. She took on a project role at headquarters and started to develop onboarding practices, which include the Base Camp program for retail. Her challenge was to make sure it was culturally right and not too focused on policies and procedures. "This was a fairly major undertaking that impacts everyone who works here—I wanted to make sure we were doing it in the right way." And at REI, the "right way" means in accordance with their values.

As Hass explained, "Prior to the Base Camp program, when someone was hired and trained, the orientation focused on the nuts and bolts." And although the nuts and bolts of any job are important, in a great workplace with Trustworthy Leaders she wanted to infuse the culture of REI into new employees so that they would truly appreciate what the organization is about. Now in Base Camp there is a greater focus on the "why" behind what people do on the floor and how this is different than a job anywhere else. "Our members care a lot about

REI, and they want to interact with somebody who gets it. We really focus on our core purpose."

Store managers and department leaders deliver much of Base Camp's content. This was an intentional part of the design, as it gives leaders who are visible and frequently interacting with employees the opportunity to talk about REI's values and how they themselves seek to live up to them. As Base Camp instructors they are able to establish relationships with many people whom they see in the store yet do not directly supervise. "It's an opportunity for a leader to share what's important to him or her with the team," Hass said. It's also an invaluable opportunity to develop skills as a Trustworthy Leader. Base Camp sessions provide people with time and opportunities to reflect on personal and company values and to consider those times when living by their values benefited themselves and others.

The Base Camp experience is extended to senior leaders as well. The design of specific orientation activities ensures that senior leaders responsible for broad areas of the company are also steeped in the company's values and the "why" behind REI's practices. Hass explained, "It goes all the way up to the vice president, CEO, and CFO. We've designed some specific things for executives that are slightly different than what an individual contributor might get, more in depth." Leading at REI is very different from working in a public company, and if a new leader comes in at the executive level and tries to lead in the same way as at a public company, it's not going to work. Base Camp experiences help them to understand what's different and the actions they might take to lead differently, to explore, and build trust. Base Camp helps new leaders at REI to develop their Virtuous Circle with an REI flair to it.

Stephanie Fischer, also introduced in Chapter Two, works with Hass to customize the onboarding process for leaders. She described some of the efforts that help senior leaders acculturate to the values at REI: "We spend more time in advance designing a customized training plan for new senior leaders—thinking about the relationships individual leaders will have—whom they need to know and what their position might entail. What do they need? How much do they need to learn about the culture of the organization versus the immediate tasks and challenges that will be coming their way? Especially if people come in from the outside, we want to create ways that they can demonstrate an awareness and practice of the values early on. That's important to their success and the success of REI."

This customized onboarding work is paying off significantly. REI has met or exceeded its profit expectations over the years, including in 2009, one of the worst years in retail. Yet that's not why all of this work is taken on. The core values are taught at REI because people there are fundamentally connected to these values as a way to live their lives—and this clarity about what is important simplifies things for people. Time at work, for most people at REI, is no different in terms of the values followed than time spent with family or friends or in the community. It's all based on the same fundamental human values that create trust.

REI CEO Sally Jewell recognizes that it takes a special individual to meet the leadership expectations placed on people at REI. "To [be a leader] requires a certain comfort with vulnerability. On every team I've worked with over my career, you see different levels of confidence and competence in many areas of the business. It's true here. There are areas where I have real competence, and there are areas where I am absolutely not the right person. Many CEOs in particular think that they need to know more or be better than the people that work with them, which is just not the case. A lot of our success depends on how comfortable leaders are in their own skin at every level of the organization."

Jewell spoke of the shifting landscape of leadership practice that she sees not only in the United States, but also around the world. "Some people are leaders from a different time in history, and I don't just mean in terms of age, I mean in terms of style. [The style] used to be command and control, you tell people what to do, you are in charge, and you are decisive whether or not you're wrong. That's not who I am or who I've ever been." Jewell is clear about who she is as a leader in part because of her ability to reflect on what is important to her—there are many moments from her past that she uses to guide her actions in the future.

When REI opened up a store in Japan, they created an environment that was very different from how people were used to working. Jewell believes that people really appreciated that, both men and women. As she said, "I believe more people want to work for a company that has a strong purpose. Those things evolve and some organizations and individuals are more in the right place at the right time than others."

Jewell would say that the future of REI's values is in the hands of every employee and co-op member. Yet she also is very clear about the significant responsibility that she holds for ensuring that the founding values are understood by all and that actions tied to the values are reinvigorated to meet the needs of a changing world. She is explicit about the importance of being visible and, as related in the first chapter, she is clear on the nonnegotiables of leadership at REI.

Jewell reinforces the nonnegotiables through her own actions, and those actions provide guidance to others. People see her put the company's values into practice and experience clarity through her example. I actually watched an interaction after my interview with Jewell that, upon reflection, became a defining moment that helped me to understand more deeply the culture of this company.

After my conversation with Jewell ended, I was standing in the hallway outside of her office, waiting for the person who had been helping me find my way to various meetings. I looked up at the sound of a rolling cart and saw an older man walking toward me, pushing a large trash container ahead of him. I moved out of the way, which placed me beside a column in the hallway.

As he got closer, I also noticed out of the corner of my eye that Jewell was coming down the hallway from the other direction to go into the lobby and greet the next person she needed to meet. As these two people approached each other—the CEO of the company and an employee with custodial responsibilities—Jewell looked up with a smile

on her face and said, "Hey Wayne, nice to see you, how are you doing?"
To which Wayne replied, with a smile, "Hi Sally, I'm doing just fine."

Jewell then headed down the stairs to meet her guest, oblivious
to the fact that I was watching. Wayne Frantz, a Corporate
Services team member, did see me. And as he walked by, he stood up
a little straighter and gave me a beaming smile that conveyed to me
the intense sense of belonging that he had just experienced in that
brief interaction. That small gesture that affirmed his value as a human
being was evidence of Sally Jewell's Virtuous Circle put into action, in a brief moment in time.

> REI truly lives its core values and encourages all
> of us to do the same to gain happiness, health,
> and pride. I always get the feeling that REI bases
> its business decisions on "How will this affect our
> employees and our co-op members?"
> —*REI employee*

DOING WHAT FEELS RIGHT

At Wegmans, as at Hoar and REI, leaders act from a set of values
known and understood by all. The leaders—and the company as a
whole—operate within a Virtuous Circle that extends beyond the
boundaries of the workplace, reaching into the community. During the
past four years, leaders at Wegmans have made a series of decisions
that brought with them notable short-term financial costs, yet set the
stage for the continued extraordinary success of this ninety-five-year-old
grocery store chain. Their bold decisions, deeply rooted in the firm's
mission, values, and beliefs, exemplify the power of Trustworthy
Leadership and provide examples that we can all learn from.

On January 4, 2008, Wegmans—which employs over thirty-nine
thousand people in seventy-five stores throughout the northeastern
United States—shocked many people by declaring that they would stop
selling all tobacco products in their stores. They set a final "quit" date
of February 10, 2008, giving their stores a window of about one month

to sell out the inventory on hand, and giving customers notification of this change. Employees, of course, were also notified, as was the general public. Most everyone responded positively, though many in the grocery industry questioned the wisdom of delisting a product that brought in significant revenue.

The American Lung Association praised Wegmans in editorials and press releases, and awarded them the Lung Champion Award in recognition of the enormity of the decision, while *Ethisphere* magazine named Danny Wegman one of the 100 Most Influential People in Business Ethics for 2008. Internally the reaction was swift and positive—from smokers and nonsmokers alike. Wegmans had previously established a QuitNet program to help employees quit smoking, and within days of the announcement in 2008, over nine hundred people —employees and spouses—enrolled in the program. To date, over 2,500 employees have signed up for the program at a cost, covered by Wegmans, of over $350,000.

And what about the financial impact of not selling cigarettes and other tobacco-related products? A round estimate of $1 million of lost revenue per year is talked about, yet it is not seen as a loss. As CEO Danny Wegman explains, the action was simply an effort to be consistent with the values they want to live by. "We believe that there is not a bad food. You can eat too much of any food, but it's not a bad food. We don't believe that cake is a bad food; you just don't want to eat that much cake. But we don't believe that there is any good cigarette." And the recognition that there is no "good" cigarette is what moved the leaders at Wegmans to stop selling tobacco products.

Danny explained, "What we like to do generally is start with our own people. There are thirty-eight thousand or thirty-nine thousand of us now, and we say, 'What is good for us?' If it is good for us, it will be good for our customers, too. We reached a point where we were wondering how we could encourage our own employees to be healthy while we were selling cigarettes. And that was when we decided to stop." The question arose in the middle of a meeting among the senior executive team: "How can we sell cigarettes to people when we don't believe there

is a good cigarette?" It was a significant question, one that many executive teams at other stores have failed to consider. The subsequent decision to stop selling cigarettes was swift. A strong Virtuous Circle will
bring with it a sense of clarity that propels bold decisions.

Many people outside of Wegmans persisted in pointing to the risk
of "lost" revenue in a low-margin industry like food retailing. Yet
Danny's response was both calm and philosophical. "It doesn't really
matter," he said. "I mean, was it a loss or was it a gain, to do the right
thing? It just came back to that. I think what surprised us about the
decision was the number of comments that we did get about doing the
right thing. I know I was surprised." Inside Wegmans people automati-
cally said, "Of course." It's the right thing to do—there was no question. It took a half-hour discussion within the company, and leaders
decided it was the right thing. The public reaction was the surprising
thing. As Danny says, "Two years later we still get comments and questions like, 'Why did you do it? What a risky decision,' and even our
friends in the industry reacted like, 'Wow, is everything going all right
with that?'"

Colleen Wegman, president since 2007, concurred with Danny's
thoughts and expressed her confidence that in doing the right thing,
the company would continue to be fine. "We all have a competitive
spirit," she said, "especially when it comes to supporting our efforts to
do what is right. We'll make that million dollars, we'll find ways to help
customers, and we'll do it better. We'll figure it out."

Interestingly, none of the external questioning of the decision concerned whether or not the decision was "right." It focused instead on
the potential loss in revenue. Wegmans executive team, however,
focused first on what was right and then on how to ensure that the
lost revenue could be turned around to be a success for the organization. As Danny said, "We've always been committed to doing the right
thing. And the more success you have at doing it, it just reinforces it.
So I can't think of a pivotal time, but there have been a number of
things, like with the cigarettes, where we would take a stand and it
would work."

There are many examples that back up Danny's words. Later in 2008, as gas prices increased dramatically, the cost of many basic products and services also increased. Companies frequently passed on these increases to consumers, which made life harder for many people. Not at Wegmans.

"Last year in June [2008]," said Danny, "things kept getting worse—the gas prices were flying up to $4.00 a gallon, and our prices were being driven up by ethanol prices. It put our employees in a terrible spot, because they had to drive to work, and their food prices were going up as well. We weren't having a great year, and we were thinking, 'What can we do for these people?'" What they did was give their employees discount cards that they could use for six weeks to receive 10 percent off all of their purchases. Danny's comments reflect his primary focus on the impact that the price increases were having on employees. That's what wasn't going well, and leaders at Wegmans responded by putting their values first.

Following on their initial response to the worsening economy, Wegmans took a few more steps that again reinforced the connection between being trustworthy, doing the right thing, and business success. The economy continued to tumble from late 2008 into 2009, with the cost of goods rising and more people facing economic difficulties.

"Our customers were having terrible problems, and we hedged the wrong way in oil and gas. We run our own bakeries, and we hedged the wrong way on flour," Danny said. "We knew that costs were going to come down by February, so back in November we decided to bring our prices down . . . to the extent that, for our business, it was around a $12 million reduction [relative to what the products might have sold for]. We were also anticipating a 3 percent wage increase for our people, and asking, "'Wow, is that the right thing to do? Do we have the money to spend?'" Not that the focus at Wegmans was on trying to save money as a company, yet in every organization money and profit are necessary to ensure that employees have jobs. At Wegmans the number one concern was to ensure that people would have jobs.

As Danny related this series of events and the choices facing the executive team, every decision, every option considered came back to values and the honorable leadership practices that leaders use. They decided to go ahead with the wage increase, reinstated the 10-percent discount card for the holidays, and lowered prices in the pharmacy and on other products. "There was $15 million [for the wage increase], and then a little later we spent another $15 million lowering pharmacy prices. It was quite emotional how our employees felt about these things." By their estimates, close to $60 million was spent on these programs to support employees and customers in times of need.

"Why am I saying this?" he asks. "Because if we have a flat year and we just spent $60 million—well, we are nervous. But we thought it was the right thing to do, and that's how we run the company. In retrospect, our business has been very strong, and we made up that money. That's why I am saying this—if you really pay attention to both your customers and your people, it seems to work out. And I think that everybody gets it: doing the right thing is important."

He adds that if you don't continue to reinforce doing the right thing, you can lose the connection between values and success. Wegmans has been reinforcing it for years, and both Danny and Colleen talk about the connection they experience on a daily basis with the past and the future. The past very often is represented by words and stories involving Robert Wegman—their father and grandfather, respectively— who always talked about taking care of employees and taking care of customers as the primary reasons to be in business.

When he took over the grocery store in the 1950s, one of his first acts was to raise the wages of employees, because he didn't believe that people could live fairly on the wages they were currently being paid. This was probably one of the earliest "livable wage" actions ever taken—without sanctions, protests, or new minimum wage laws being passed. Robert Wegman did it because he felt it was the right thing to do, an action that now can be studied as a defining moment in the development of his Virtuous Circle. And this same process of taking action continues with the decisions made by Danny, Colleen, and other leaders at Wegmans as they move into the future.

Do Danny and Colleen simply have soft hearts, helping them to miraculously find success where others have been unable to do so? No. Danny and Colleen Wegman are very smart people who help to lead a very successful business in a tough industry with significant competition. They are aware of the importance of ensuring that the business is profitable, and their approach to success focuses on the operations of the entire business—the physical structure of the stores, the quality of the products and services, the people who work there, and the people who come to shop there. And it is the people who come first, because without them nothing else would exist.

"The good news about the Wegmans story is that it does work. I get up and pinch myself every day—it's true—it does work. If it didn't work, you couldn't stick with it," Danny said. "These are things that aren't taught in business schools. They will teach you the techniques of financial analysis, which are ridiculous most of the time. The fact that this has worked for us over a period of time . . . we just feel better and better and better about it. We're so blessed that we treat each other the way we want to be treated and it does work, and we say 'Wahoo, let's do more of that!' If you talk about a Virtuous Circle, I think that's kind of where we are."

Treating people the way you want to be treated yourself works. That is what our company is a testimony to—we do it for ourselves, not to show anyone else, yet it works. And we are so happy that it does. I mean, what if getting up every day and being grumpy and yelling at people and whipping them proves to be a great financial success and you thought that was the model? Who would want to live like that? Gosh, did you win?

—*Danny Wegman, CEO*

Colleen Wegman, following in her father's and grandfather's footsteps, has a long successful future ahead of herself strengthening her own Virtuous Circle as a Trustworthy Leader. Although her father describes the lessons from his defining moments with the phrase "Do the right thing," Colleen's term is "Do what feels right in your heart." Other people who work at Wegmans have their own versions of this stance. Everyone gets to do what's right, and it works.

CREATING YOUR OWN VIRTUOUS CIRCLE

In the process of writing this book, I had a chance to see firsthand what happens in organizations when the power of the Virtuous Circle is fully unleashed. I met and interviewed many great leaders, and by listening to their stories and reflecting on their experiences, I've deepened my understanding of trust and trustworthy behavior.

When leaders practice integrity toward the values supporting honor and inclusion, engage their followers, share information, and develop others, they then are able to move through uncertainty with grace and determination. Their ability to turn uncertainty into opportunity can be seen in the great high-performing organizations profiled throughout this book.

Trustworthy Leaders *know* that being trustworthy is the critical factor that separates their leadership success from that of others. Interestingly, these leaders don't worry about *proving* that being trustworthy makes a powerful difference or leads to better results. They know that what they are doing is right and beneficial, so they keep doing it. They want to understand the impact of trust and how they can strengthen this aspect of their leadership, yet they know that understanding and proving are two different things.

Every organization profiled in this book collects data on the activities they engage in that leaders believe create a positive, trust-filled workplace. And every one of these organizations dedicates tremendous resources to enhancing people's ability to be trustworthy. Yet none of the leaders with whom I spoke indicated any compulsion to prove cause and effect. They are guided by the evidence that they see and experience for themselves. The data they collect—both quantitative and qualitative—helps them to assess, evaluate, and improve. They move forward with what they know and what works over time, often course correcting and always seeking improvement.

The positive financial impact that comes from being trustworthy is seen in markers such as low turnover, high numbers of job applicants, reduced employee stress, greater customer or patient satisfaction, and greater creativity. Leaders accept the fact that trust works, and this acceptance saves them and their organizations the time and money that others spend unendingly searching for the magic formula that might prove that one program versus another will guarantee a specific increase in profit. Trustworthy Leadership is profitable because the collective power and creativity of a unified group of people working toward common goals while sharing respect and benefits with all is unbeatable.

While writing this book, I also affirmed something I've seen in many organizations—Trustworthy Leaders know and appreciate the virtue of *simplicity*, which pervades a number of their practices. People are different, of course, and have different needs. Yet Trustworthy Leaders take a simple—not simplistic—approach to people: they treat everyone from the same baseline of honor and inclusion. Simplicity also supports leaders' efforts to minimize distractions: they pare down their organizations' core values and principles to the most important few, which are clearly articulated and distinct. Leaders often told me how helpful it was to clarify and simplify the values guiding their actions as Trustworthy Leaders.

I also learned that, among Trustworthy Leaders, perfection does not exist, and no one is aiming for it. Every leader I spoke with told stories about his or her mistakes, stumbles, humbling moments, and lessons learned. They even anticipated what they would probably continue to stumble over. Trustworthy Leaders are able to *see and accept their imperfections*, while always aspiring to the high standards they set for themselves. They know that a lack of perfection is not an excuse for doing the wrong thing; rather, it reinforces their belief that doing the right thing is an ongoing process.

Finally, I learned that Trustworthy Leaders are not as rare as you might think. They are actually very much like you and me. They have their good days and bad days. They have some skills that are extraordinary and others that aren't. And they follow their Virtuous Circle every day. At different moments in their journey their leadership practices may reflect a stronger focus on one element than on another, yet all the elements are always in play. Trustworthy Leaders live from a core set of positive values and they lead in ways that reinforce their Virtuous Circle. You can do this too.

Although Trustworthy Leaders may still be more unique than common, there are enough of them out there that, if you truly want to be one, you can find people from whom you can learn. I hope that the stories shared in this book help you understand the experiences that influenced the leadership development of each of the Trustworthy Leaders profiled. I also hope that these stories encourage you to reflect on your own experiences—those moments when you've been accepting, you've fostered simplicity, you've moved beyond a search for perfection. My wish is that you see your actions as a reflection of your own Virtuous Circle—as I do now, looking back on my adventurous night hike. Let trust be your guide.

NOTES

Chapter 1

1. R. Levering, M. Moskowitz, and M. Katz, *The 100 Best Companies to Work for in America* (Reading, MA: Addison-Wesley, 1984).

2. R. Levering, *A Great Place to Work: What Makes Some Employers So Good (and Most So Bad)* (New York: Random House, 1988).

3. Russell Investment Group, *Stock-Market Performance of Fortune "Best 100 Companies to Work for in America,"* January 2011, http://www.greatplacetowork.com/what_we_believe/graphs.php.

Chapter 3

1. "E Pluribus Unum: Diversity and Community in the Twenty-first Century," *Scandinavian Political Studies*, *30*(2). In the abstract, Putnam states: "In the long run immigration and diversity are likely to have important cultural, economic, fiscal, and developmental benefits. In the short run, however, immigration and ethnic diversity tend to reduce social solidarity and social capital. New evidence from the US suggests that in ethnically diverse neighbourhoods residents of all races tend to 'hunker down.' Trust (even of one's own race) is lower, altruism and community cooperation rarer, friends fewer. In the long run, however, successful immigrant societies have overcome such fragmentation by creating new, cross-cutting forms of social solidarity and more encompassing identities."

2. Scott Page, *The Difference: How the Power of Diversity Creates Better Groups, Firms, Schools and Societies* (Princeton, NJ: Princeton University Press, 2007), 375.

3. Amy Lyman, "Creating Trust: It's Worth the Effort," Great Place to Work Institute White Paper, San Francisco, CA, 2008, updated 2011.

4. Coie Perkins, *Diversity 2009 Year in Review.*

Chapter 4

1. Warren Bennis, "Followership," *USC Business*, Spring 1994.

2. Michael McKinney, "Leadership and Followership," interview with Alexander Haslam and Stephen Reicher, *Vision: Insights and New Horizons*, Winter 2008.

Chapter 6

1. Robert K. Greenleaf, *The Servant as Leader* (Westfield, IN: Robert K. Greenleaf Center, 1991; Robert K. Greenleaf, 1970), p. 7.

2. Ibid.

Chapter 7

1. Jonah Lehrer, "How Uncertainty Cripples Us," *Wall Street Journal,* January 8, 2011, p. C12.

ACKNOWLEDGMENTS

There are always many people's contributions to recognize when you are presenting something that reflects many years of work—and that is the case with this book. Given that I've written a lot about the experiences that shaped the trustworthy leaders in my book, I also have many experiences that I could acknowledge as influential to my own development and the development of the ideas I've shared here. For reasons of space and time, I'm limiting my comments here, and will include more stories and thank-yous on my website, www .trustworthyleader.org.

I give a deep thank-you to everyone who consented to be interviewed for this book. I appreciate your willingness to share your time and your stories with me and to allow me to share your stories with others.

I thank the people at Jossey-Bass who have supported this and other projects with the Institute. In particular, Genoveva Llosa's editorial contributions, Lisa Shannon's many conversations, and Holly Allen's interest in developing companion training materials have all kept things moving forward. We have shared intense discussions and pushed through challenges to keep things on track. My work is better because of their support. I also thank Jenna Free and Kristi Hein for their thoughtful editing, helping me to convey my ideas more clearly and succinctly.

I thank the people with whom I've worked at the Institute for so many years and those of you who have moved on to other positions as well. What we started at the Institute was built on a desire to change the world. People came together, worked hard, shared their ideas and laughter, and created a spirit of togetherness that was quite compelling to all of us and to the companies and people with whom we worked.

There are many names to mention—Sarah, Erika, Michael, Hal, Suzanne, Jen, Brooke, Todd, Ann, Marcus, Jessica, and others—people I've worked with for years, who helped me to learn and grow. I think of you all often.

I also thank the people at Neteor who worked with me for years, developing phenomenal web-based tools that enabled me to sort through reams of data that used to make my eyes glaze over. I never would have been able to sift through all the employee survey, culture audit, and employee comment records without the brilliant help of people at Neteor.

I want to thank my father for inspiring me always, for challenging me to look at the consequences of my actions, and for supporting me even when he didn't fully understand what I was doing and why. I want to thank Helen O'Bannon and Tom Ehrlich for being role models for me so many years ago, encouraging me to stick up for what I thought was right and to speak out on issues of importance to me. I want to thank Marc Simon for giving me so much of his time and care, for talking over ideas that were just barely formed, for always, always encouraging me to write, and for his heartbeat. I want to thank Simeon, my amazing son, for giving me so many gifts and sticking with me as we go forward. He is my inspiration for creating a better world for everyone.

ABOUT THE AUTHOR

Amy Lyman is a cofounder of the Great Place to Work Institute. During her tenure she developed the Institute's consulting services in the United States, and oversaw the financial, legal, and operational activities of the entire organization. She served as president of the Institute for a time and as chair of the board of directors, leaving that role in 2008.

During the past few years she has studied the qualities that distinguish Best Companies from good companies, focusing on the role of the Trustworthy Leader. She has written numerous articles on this topic and has been a featured speaker at management workshops and conferences. Honesty and integrity are central to her work.

Amy received her Ph.D. from the University of Pennsylvania and her B.S. from the University of California, Davis.

Prior to founding the Great Place to Work Institute, Amy taught classes in organization development, systems theory, and qualitative research methods in the Department of Applied Behavioral Sciences at the University of California, Davis. She began her consulting work while a research fellow at the Wharton Center for Applied Research at the University of Pennsylvania, and was a founding board member of the Family Firm Institute.

The Great Place to Work Institute is a global research and consulting firm headquartered in San Francisco, with thirty-two affiliates in

Europe, the Americas, Asia, and Oceana. The Institute uses its Trust Index employee survey and Culture Audit to produce the *Fortune* 100 Best Companies to Work For and the Best Small & Medium Companies to Work For in America lists, in addition to best companies lists in forty countries. The Institute recognizes the world's best workplaces and provides conferences, workshops, and advisory and consulting services to those who seek to create great workplaces of their own.

For over twenty years, the Institute has been conducting research into the best workplaces in the United States and around the world, and through this research has amassed a sizable body of knowledge about the characteristics, similarities and differences, cross-cultural variations, and practices that support great workplaces.

INDEX